Real C
Facts About:
Rock 'n' Roll

CRANE HILL
PUBLISHERS

Real Cheesy Facts About: Rock 'n' Roll

Copyright © 2006 by Crane Hill Publishers

ISBN-13: 978-1-57587-251-3
ISBN-10: 1-57587-251-X

Book design by Miles G. Parsons
Illustrations by Neal Cross and Miles G. Parsons

Printed in the United States of America

Library of Congress Cataloging-in-Publication Data

Platt, Camille Smith.
  Real cheesy facts about-- rock stars / by Camille Smith Platt.
      p. cm.
  ISBN-13: 978-1-57587-251-3
  1. Rock musicians--Anecdotes. 2. Rock musicians--Miscellanea. I. Title.

ML394.P59 2006
781.66092'2--dc22

2006024893

Real Cheesy Facts About: Rock 'n' Roll

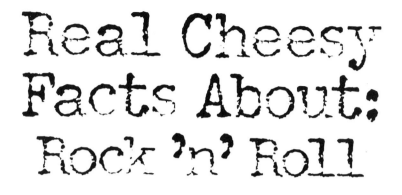

Camille Smith Platt

CRANE HILL
PUBLISHERS

TABLE OF CONTENTS

Chapter 1

★

Divas: Rock Stars' Wacky Habits and Demands

BERRY

Divas: Rock Stars' Wacky Habits and Demands

★ ★ ★ ★ ★ ★ ★ ★ ★ ★ ★ ★ ★ ★ ★ ★

Just what is it that brings out the wild side in rockers on tour? Is it the lyrics and the screaming groupies, or is it simply boredom from so many weeks on the road? Or maybe their crazy antics are publicity ploys, as they try anything to maintain their stardom. Whether it's going nuts onstage, shooting off their mouths on late-night talk shows, or making wacky demands to the people trying to please them, these artists are nothing short of divas.

Prince demands to have a physician inject him with Vitamin B12 before each of his shows. He also requires all food located backstage remain covered with cellophane until he can uncover each item.

★ ★ ★ ★ ★

Break Stuff–Bad Backstage Behavior

When it came to finding innovative ways to look badass on tour, The Who was unbeatable. The first band to make smashing instruments onstage cool, they were infamous for their mess-making ways. Drummer Keith Moon first tossed his drums around during his audition with fellow band mates. The trend stuck, and the adrenaline rush of destroying something so expensive, in front of a crowd so loud, was contagious. Guitarist Pete Townshend quickly caught on, and front man Roger Daltrey started swinging his microphone over his head. Townshend, however, claims his first guitar-busting incident was actually an accident when it was smacked by a low ceiling fan at an indoor club. Regardless, the rocker legend of shattering pricey gear lives on.

Other Rock Stars Who Smashed Their Stuff

Kurt Cobain—Grunge bands like Pearl Jam often took after Nirvana's Kurt Cobain and vented their frustration by smashing their guitars.

Jimi Hendrix—The king of playing guitar in the most terribly uncomfortable positions (with his teeth and between his legs), Hendrix first got violent onstage when he smashed his guitar to bits at the Monterey International Pop Festival in 1967.

★ ★ ★ ★ ★

CRAZY (AND INTOXICATED)

Smashing stuff onstage may be a rush to some famous rockers, but others prefer to keep it in the privacy of their own hotel rooms. **An infamous pair often nicknamed the "Toxic Twins," Steven Tyler and Joe Perry of Aerosmith, had their fair share of drug problems** in the 1970s, and thanks to cabin fever brought on by being on the road for months at a time, they quickly developed a fetish for destruction. To keep them busy in their hotel rooms after concerts, Tyler and Perry always took two staples on tour with them: chainsaws and extra-long extension cords. Why? Because

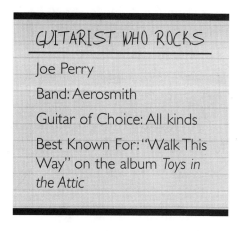

GUITARIST WHO ROCKS

Joe Perry

Band: Aerosmith

Guitar of Choice: All kinds

Best Known For: "Walk This Way" on the album *Toys in the Attic*

they wanted to do as much damage as possible. The chainsaws were used to slice up the hotel room. The cords were used when they tossed the television out of the hotel window, so they could watch their favorite shows all the way down.

Aerosmith wasn't the only band to trash its temporary living quarters while on tour. While in Germany in 1984, **Mötley Crüe tossed mattresses out of their windows** because they thought the mattresses would look cool bouncing off the cars below. The government didn't put up with such antics for long, though—the band was tossed out of the country within the week. Keith Moon of

The Who, nicknamed "Moon the Loon," was also infamous for making a mess. When a hotel manager asked him to turn down his noisy tunes one afternoon (which happened to be a cassette of his own music), Moon tore his room to shreds and said, "That was noise." Restarting his tape, he continued, "This is The Who."

★ ★ ★ ★ ★

THIS USED TO BE MY PLAYGROUND

A shock-value pop idol who loves to push the envelope with her edgy lyrics and constant reinvention of image, Madonna was a little star-struck (and jealous) when Anaheim skater chick Gwen Stefani emerged in Hollywood from the ska music scene. Since opening for industry veterans Red Hot Chili Peppers and rock reggae star Ziggy Marley in the early 1990s, No Doubt had struggled to earn their fame. As the band continued to push for recognition and their first hits, "Just

CELEBRITY ALIAS

Alias: Ziggy Marley
Actual Name: David Marley

A Girl" and "Spiderwebs," climbed the charts, Stefani stole the spotlight from the Material Girl and became increasingly popular for her rock-hard midriff and eastern bindi jewel. Taking a bit of a backseat to the newbie, Madonna was rumored to have called Stefani a poser for copying Madonna's signature dance moves and hairstyles.

"Just A Girl" was not the first music video No Doubt ever made for MTV. As the band struggled for recognition in the early 1990s, they sent producers a low-budget video for the single "Trapped in the Box," but MTV didn't air it once.

Soon after the comment, Madonna's long-time friend Rosie O'Donnell canceled Stefani's upcoming appearance on her talk show. O'Donnell claimed it was because of "scheduling differences," but No Doubt fans suspected it was a friendly favor.

★ ★ ★ ★ ★

AIN'T TOO PROUD TO BEG (FOR FORGIVENESS)

DID YOU KNOW

Madonna is distantly related to both Gwen Stefani and Celine Dion.

A rock and roll legend dating back to hits such as "Roll Over Beethoven" (1956) and "Johnny B. Goode" (1958), **Chuck Berry is used to getting what he wants.** Known for never sharing the spotlight, Berry always toured by himself and required venues to provide a backup band at each concert. His demanding ways embarrassed him at the Hollywood Palladium Theatre in 1972, however. The concert was rockin' until his lead guitarist suddenly let someone else take his place on stage. Confused about the switch, Berry stopped in the middle of a song to complain that the replacement was playing

too loud and drowning out his vocals. Later, he blushed when he realized that the swap was a surprise appearance by Rolling Stones legend Keith Richards.

★ ★ ★ ★ ★

This Is A Rebel Chick

More famous for her buzz cut than for her actual talent as an artist, Irish pop singer **Sinead O'Connor was the queen of attitude and anti-patriotism.** In 1990, she turned down an offer to play a gig in New Jersey because she didn't want to support any event where the national anthem would be played. Later that year, while shopping

at a health food store in California, she allegedly had an employee fired for playing the tune overhead to get on her nerves.

O'Connor's most famous anti-everything escapade was, of course, when she finally agreed to appear on Saturday Night Live in 1992. (She had refused the first offer in 1990 because she did not want to appear with comedian Andrew Clay, who she said was too edgy.) As O'Connor began her opening monologue, however, producers quickly regretted the second offer. Instead of spouting off the expected one-liners, O'Connor sang the Bob Marley song "War" and tore up a photo of Pope John Paul II.

> ### THE EARLY YEARS
> While Sinead O'Connor was a student at Dublin College of Music, she earned money by dressing up as a French maid and giving Kiss-o-grams.

★ ★ ★ ★ ★

IF YOU WANNA BE MY PRODUCER—YOU'VE GOTTA GET WITH MY DEMANDS

When Posh Spice Victoria Adams and soccer hunk hubby, David Beckham, got the news that a British television station wanted to film a documentary about their ultra-extravagant lives, they did what any star would do—they got picky and took over. Not only did the couple want complete control over censoring private or potentially embarrassing video segments they might want deleted from the documentary, they also demanded the right to fire anyone they didn't like during the filming. Program producers decided Adams and Beckham were a little too demanding and soon canceled the project. A documentary was made, and a DVD version of *The Real Beckhams* was released in 2003.

★ ★ ★ ★ ★

PSYCHED FOR PSEUDONYMS

Changing their name is something bored rock stars have always been delighted to do, so long as their fans comply. Hoping to reinvent himself (over and over again), **David Jones of Brixton, England, thought his name was too dorky**—and too similar to cheesy heartthrob Davy Jones of the Monkees. So he changed his name to Lou. Then he changed it to Calvin. Then, after being inspired by a very sharp (and very manly) Bowie knife, he changed it once and for all to David Bowie. No stranger to identity crisis, Bowie has since been known by an assortment of other alter egos, including Ziggy Stardust, Aladdin Sane, and Thin White Duke.

More famous for changing his name (and his funky purple outfits) than anyone, however, is the wacky artist formerly known as Prince. While his weirdest (and most unpronounceable) change was back in 1993 with the perplexing squiggle—which looked something like the overlapped symbols for

CELEBRITY ALIAS

Alias: Prince
Actual Name: Prince Rogers Nelson

male and female—he has a history of silly pseudonyms that include Joey Coco, Jamie Starr, Alexander Nevermind, and, who could forget, His Royal Badness (because he likes to think that he is "bad" in the same way that Michael Jackson was "Bad," meaning good).

★ ★ ★ ★ ★

BOTTOMS UP

Friends and musicians **Gibby Haynes and Paul Leary had trouble deciding what to call themselves** before landing on this ingenious name The Butthole Surfers. In their early years, the band gave themselves a new name for every show they played—Abe Lincoln's Bush, the Dave Clark Five, the Vodka Family Winstons, and a long list of other ridiculous monikers.

Students at Trinity University in Texas, Haynes and Leary started their own business selling pillowcases and T-shirts decorated with pictures of Lee Harvey Oswald.

While many bands made the bad move of converting their stardom to the small screen as video game protagonists, Gary Garcia and Jerry Buckner paid tribute to classics such as *Pac-Man, Donkey Kong,* and *Centipede* through music. After their first single, "Pac-Man Fever," climbed the Billboard Top 40 in the early 1980s, they decided to create a whole album based on video games. Its most memorable songs include "Do the Donkey Kong" and "Ode to a Centipede."

★ ★ ★ ★ ★

WHO'S BAD?

When KISS kicked onto the music scene in the 1970s, they were instantly famous for their heavy metal pyrotechnics and outrageous makeup. A symbol of all things rebellious (and sometimes satanic), the band's live shows and albums were a huge success. Longing for even more fame and fortune, they asked themselves, "Could we make fans out of video gamers?" Not quite.

> ### CELEBRITY ALIAS
>
> Alias: Gene Simmons
> Actual Name: Chaim Witz

During the band's comeback tour in the 1990s, they noticed that vintage KISS pinball machines had become a collectible in high demand, and decided to market the game for home computers and Nintendo systems. The idea bombed, but the band didn't lose heart—they released a *second* video game even more horrible than the first called *Psycho Circus*, which also bombed just as miserably.

Gene Simmons wasn't the only rock legend to flop when he tried to take his tunes to the gaming realm. **Featuring cheesy musical synthesizer versions of "Beat It" and "Billie Jean,"** Michael Jackson's *Moonwalker* game for Sega Genesis hit stores in 1989. The premise: defeat kidnappers and drug dealers and rescue children around the world while wearing a stylin' zoot suit and holding funky dance-offs in graveyards and dark closets.

★ ★ ★ ★ ★

PROVOKING THE PISTOLS

The Sex Pistols never set out to fire off a round of curse words on an evening talk show in the U.K. in 1976, but after the band was provoked by interviewer Bill Grundy to "step outside," every British kiddie up past their bedtime had several crude new additions to their vocabulary. Initially brought on to tell late-night viewers about the underground punk movement, the Pistols' interview was quite peaceful at first. They were actually charming (if a little over-dressed). Possibly disappointed that he couldn't reveal the rockers as talentless metal heads, Grundy laid on the vague insults and finally snapped, "You've got another ten seconds, say something outrageous." Vocalist Steve Jones gave him what he asked for. A few f-bombs later, England had a taste of what punk rock was all about.

CELEBRITY ALIASES

Alias: Johnny Rotten
Actual Name: John Lydon

Alias: Sid Vicious
Actual Name: John Simon Ritchie

GUITARIST WHO ROCKS

Steve Jones

Band: The Sex Pistols

Guitar of Choice: Les Paul Custom

Best Known For: "Anarchy in the U.K." from the album *Never Mind the Bollocks, Here's the Sex Pistols* (1977)

19

★ ★ ★ ★ ★

FIGHT FOR YOUR RIGHT TO RIOT

Right-wing daddies, fearing the sexual rebellion of their innocent teenage daughters, reared their ugly heads when the Beastie Boys set out to tour Great Britain in the spring of 1987. Rumor had it that the band's stage show was obscene, and that their fans were known to riot. Although exaggerated, the trepidation materialized when the rockers played their gig at the Liverpool Royal Court. Thanks to a steady rain of beer cans and tear gas lobbed into the crowd by drunken fans, the show was stopped after only ten minutes. Beastie Ad-Rock allegedly joined the madness to spite those who had predicted the trouble—he was charged with throwing a beer car in a fan's face.

★ ★ ★ ★ ★

YOU GIVE STRIPPERS A BAD NAME

After ditching his high school R&B cover band, Atlantic City Expressway, rocker **Jon Bon Jovi formed a hot New Jersey band** called Jon Bon Jovi and the Wild Ones, and hit the town with his tunes. While still too young to get into the clubs where he played every weekend, he recorded his first record at age nineteen, but it wasn't all that glamorous. His first big hit was "R2-D2, We Wish You a Merry Christmas," which he recorded for a holiday Star Wars album. The humble, cheesy beginnings would soon change.

Bon Jovi's band began acting like true rock divas when their third album rolled around, and they chose singles like "Wanted Dead or

Alive" for the album they eloquently titled *Slippery When Wet*. While the front man says they chose the title based on signs they saw on the highway, David Bryan disagreed. Bryan openly spread the rumor that the title was a tribute to striptease clubs where women would pour soapy water all over each other.

CELEBRITY ALIAS

Alias: Jon Bon Jovi
Actual Name: John Bongiovi

21

★ ★ ★ ★ ★

NICE GUYS LIGHT UP LAST

Billie Joe Armstrong and Mike Dirnt of Green Day had a slow start to fame, but like any hopeful rock star, persevered through the rough years of being no-namers. While in high school, the boys were scheduled to play a gig with the Lookouts in California. But when they got there, the power didn't work, the bathrooms were out of order, and only about five people had shown up for the party. Unscathed by the disappointment, Sweet Children—which was the name of their band at the time—plugged into a generator, lit a few candles, and rocked out. Lookouts guitarist Larry Livermore, who also ran an independent music label, offered them a record deal on the spot.

As a sixteen-year-old artist new to the punk music scene, Billie Joe Armstrong earned the nickname "Two-Dollar Bill" for selling joints for $2 each. He changed his band's name to Green Day, which is slang for spending an entire day smoking pot. His mother must have been proud.

★ ★ ★ ★ ★

REACH OUT AND TOUCH SOMEONE

Diana Ross was called Diane by friends and family until her early twenties.

When a security guard frisked soul diva Diana Ross at London's Heathrow Airport in the late 1990s, she flipped out. Upset that she had been needlessly fondled and that her complaint had not been taken seriously, Ross walked back over to the smirking guard and gave her a taste of her own medicine. Ross felt the guard's body in the same way, saying, "There, how do you like it?" Ross continued to explain that she was wearing a tight bodysuit that would have made any hidden weapon obvious—there was no need to feel her breasts and in between her legs. Ross was arrested for her retaliation. Since then, she has been no stranger to run-ins with the police. In 2002, she failed a sobriety test and was arrested for drunk driving in Arizona.

When Ross tried to organize a reunion tour with the other original members of The Supremes in the 2000s, her plea fell on deaf ears when Mary Wilson and Cindy Birdsong were only offered $3 million and $1 million, respectively. They simply could not support a tour where their ultra-famous third wheel would make so much more money than they. Ross had been offered a whopping $15 million.

★ ★ ★ ★ ★

PLAYING WITH FIRE

The Rolling Stones had no idea that they could have a party so full of booze, drugs, and women that they would actually set a New York hotel on fire during the

blackout of 1965. Hotel officials had provided candles to all of their residents, and when the bed caught on fire, no one seemed to notice until the blaze was out of control. How did the groupies handle the flames? They threw ice buckets at it, of course.

CELEBRITY ALIAS

Alias: Bill Wyman (The Rolling Stones)
Actual Name: William Perks

GUITARIST WHO ROCKS

Keith Richards
Band: The Rolling Stones
Guitar of Choice: 5-string Fender Telecaster; Fender Twin
Best Known For: "Honkey Tonk Women" on the album *Hot Rocks 1964-1971*

★ ★ ★ ★ ★

OPPORTUNITIES LOST

A rock star just wouldn't be a rock star if she didn't turn down major movie roles. All jealousy (and touring schedules) aside, Britney Spears did just that when she missed out on the opportunity to star in not one, but

five big-screen productions. *Chicago* producer Harvey Weinstein had allegedly hoped the pop queen would play the part of Kitty Baxter, which later went to actress Lucy Liu. Britney was also considered for the part of Allie in the award-winning film *The Notebook*, but newcomer Rachel McAdams won the part instead. Spears turned down small roles in *Scary Movie* and *Buffy the Vampire Slayer* because of scheduling conflicts, but her biggest loss was when Jessica Simpson beat her out in the race to play Daisy Duke in the 2005 remake of *The Dukes of Hazzard*.

Madonna has also had her fair share of roles thrown her way. She was offered roles in *Showgirls* and *Casino,* as well as Michelle Pfeiffer's part in *Batman Returns*, Jada Pinkett Smith's part in *Madagascar,* and Renee Zellwegger's part in *Chicago.*

DID YOU KNOW

Madonna has an IQ of 140, and the matron of honor at her second wedding was Stella McCartney.

★ ★ ★ ★ ★

YOU CAN'T ALWAYS GET WHAT YOU WANT

When it comes to rock stars and the things they "need," the sky is the limit for wacky demands. What does every head banger crave backstage? Australians INXS say a Ping-Pong table. Pop-R&B crossover diva Mariah Carey cannot do without a box of bendy straws. From these strange demands to others— everything from a personal masseuse to an endless supply of Captain Crunch cereal—these rock stars aren't afraid to make their requests known to all who are at their beck and call.

Aerosmith—Famous for their post-concert rendezvous with promiscuous women, Aerosmith frequently requested that a dozen clean bath towels and a massive pasta pit await them

> Aerosmith lead vocalist Steven Tyler hates it when friends call him "Steve."

after gigs (and no, it was not for eating). Band members would take turns hopping into the slimy pit and wrestling with their young female fans. The boys of summer made sure they got their snacks, too. On the first night of their first Japanese tour, they reportedly freaked out and destroyed their room backstage when the concert promoter put turkey rolls on their complimentary private buffet (the nerve!).

Van Halen—Known for one specific (and annoying) request in every concert contract, Van Halen always asks for a backstage bowl of M&Ms—with the brown ones removed, of course. If this crucial

DID YOU KNOW

Songwriter Janis Ian received hundreds of Valentine's Day cards on February 14, 1977, after releasing the Billboard No. 3 hit "At Seventeen," in which she sang about how she never received Valentines as a teenager.

detail is overlooked, the band stresses that the paperwork should have been read more carefully. Their picky appeals have turned them into sloppy businessmen, though. Van Halen actually canceled a Colorado concert in 1981 because when they showed up for rehearsal, brown M&Ms were still in the bowl. Well, that and when they set up their heavy equipment, the faulty stage sank to the ground. Frustrated, they reboarded the tour bus and went home.

Def Leppard—Most famous for the 1980s hit single "Pour Some Sugar on Me," these rockers were techno savvy. At concerts, they wanted a list of the radio frequencies used by every local police, ambulance, and fire station, so they could make sure the signals wouldn't interfere with their state-of-the-art wireless guitars. Just to be sure nothing else would ruin the show with feedback, they also

In 2005, Def Leppard held an online trivia contest and awarded the winner a candy blue Jackson JS1 Dinky guitar autographed by band members. The three "not-so-easy" questions were:

- When Vivian joined the band in 1992 after Steve Clark passed away, he was not the only ex-Whitesnake guitarist who was considered to join the band. Who was the other one? (Answer: John Sykes)
- During the recordings of "Let's Get Rocked," at what time did the band eat? (Answer: 6:00 p.m.)
- Which guitarist, who used to play with David Bowie, was the original inspiration for Joe and Phil to start their Cybernauts project? (Answer: Mick Ronson)

demanded that all stadium police and security turn off their cell phones, pagers, and walkie-talkies.

Christina Aguilera—A superstar at just seventeen years old with the hit pop song "Genie in a Bottle," and the epitome of *Girls Gone Wild* just three years later, Christina Aguilera learned early that what a girl wants backstage, she can have—organic foods, Flintstone chewable vitamins, herbal tea, chewing gum, and breath mints. She wasn't all health nut, though. Aguilera also made sure she had Oreos, chocolate chip cookies, and white bread for her pre-concert sandwiches.

Mariah Carey—If you aren't going to take a picture of the right side of Mariah Carey's face, you'd better not take one at all. When the pop diva is on a photo shoot, she's a bit picky about photographers paying attention to her "good side." Carey is known for whipping her head around or pulling hair over her left eye to hide her shortcomings when paparazzi are in view. And as for her live shows, Carey demands a healthy supply of Captain Crunch cereal *and* hires a personal towel-handler to pass her warm, dry towels as needed.

Korn—When it comes to describing the ideal backstage haven, urban heavy metal band Korn can think of only one word—it should have "vibe." They need a homey hangout that resembles a small, well-decorated apartment. And if the decorator

DID YOU KNOW

Paul Simon may have sung that there were officially fifty ways to leave your lover, but for fans he only listed five:

Slip out the back, Jack

Make a new plan, Stan

You don't need to be coy, Roy, just set yourself free

Hop on the bus, Gus

Drop off the key, Lee

(yes, decorator) plans on using fabric to "soften" the look of the walls and windows, the band kindly requests it be a fabric with some sort of pattern (nothing bland).

Britney Spears—Before the busy days of motherhood set in, Spears matured from the innocent-but-alluring Catholic schoolgirl in "Hit Me Baby One More Time" to the sexpot sound of the electronica-enhanced "Toxic." Just what did this million-dollar superstar want waiting for her backstage? A clean (and smell-free) carpet or rug, a telephone, and a massive fine slapped on anyone who made an incoming call that interrupted her pre-concert preparations.

★ ★ ★ ★ ★

MORE STRANGE BACKSTAGE DEMANDS...

Foo Fighters—White tube socks (U.S. size 10-13) and twelve cans of cranberry juice

Moby—Ten pairs of white socks and ten pairs of cotton boxers

Limp Bizkit—Dimmable lamps

Fiona Apple—Four red Fiji apples, one kiwi, and one ripe papaya

Nine Inch Nails—Two boxes of cornstarch

Axl Rose of Guns N' Roses—White bread and Dom Perignon champagne

Jennifer Lopez—A white room with white flowers, white couches, white candles, white curtains, and white tables (with white tablecloths, of course)

Jennifer Lopez moved to Manhattan from the Bronx to learn how to dance and used to sleep in the studio where she practiced.

DID YOU KNOW

Nine Inch Nail's entire 2005 U.S. Club tour sold out in less than 10 minutes. Some tickets sold for more than $200 on eBay.

★ ★ ★ ★ ★

OTHER ROCKERS WITH BAD FORM:

Axl Rose of Guns N' Roses once beat up a man having a drink in a hotel bar for telling him he looked like Jon Bon Jovi.

Donnie Wahlberg of New Kids on the Block dumped vodka in the hallway of a Louisville, Kentucky, hotel and lit it on fire.

Keith Moon once trampled his neighbor's manicured tree garden with his motorcycle.

At **Madonna's** wedding to actor Sean Penn, Penn got so upset with the noise and invasion of privacy from press helicopters flying overhead that he shot at them.

GUITARIST WHO ROCKS

Slash

Band: Guns N Roses

Guitar of Choice: '85 Gibson Les Paul standard with a Crybaby wah-wah

Best Known For: "Sweet Child O' Mine" on the album *Appetite for Destruction*

New Kids on the Block was originally called Nyunk. Inspired by a rap song Donnie Wahlberg wrote for their debut album, they changed it and eventually shortened it to just NKOTB.

WHAT BIG STARS NAME THEIR BABIES: IT'S A GIRL!

- August (Garth Brooks)
- Calico (Alice Cooper)
- Carmella (Munky from Korn)
- Chastity (Cher)
- Dandelion (Keith Richards)
- Diva Muffin and Moon Unit (Frank Zappa)
- Dusty Rain (Vanilla Ice)
- Fly (Erykah Badu)
- Fuchsia (Sting)
- Lourdes (Madonna and Guy Ritchie)
- Memphis Eve (Bono from U2)
- Paris Michael Katherine (Michael Jackson)
- Phoenix Chi (Melanie "Scary Spice" Brown)
- Zoe Moon (Lenny Kravitz)

Chapter 2

I Fought the Law (and the Law Won): Famous Lawsuits

I Fought the Law (and the Law Won): Famous Lawsuits

★ ★ ★ ★ ★ ★ ★ ★ ★ ★ ★ ★ ★ ★ ★

It's not surprising that artists as famous as Metallica, The Beatles, and The Doors get tangled up in a confusing web of accusations and court battles from time to time. When you're a genius, everyone thinks they had the right to your brilliance before you did. When a song like "How Deep Is Your Love?" became a major hit, every struggling songwriter who ever attempted to write a song with the word "love" in it got a little upset that they didn't get any props from the Bee Gees. But when rock halls start accusing sub-par websites of stealing logos, and entire cities catch stars dumping their toilets into public waterways, you know things have gotten a little out of hand. Here is a synopsis of the most cheesy, and most popular, rock-star lawsuits of all time.

LIKE A BAT OUT OF HELL

Meat Loaf sued his former writing partner, Jim Steinman, for using the phrase "Bat out of Hell," from his 1977 album. Meat Loaf claims he owns the phrase in a musical context, even though he didn't actually write the song.

★ ★ ★ ★ ★

DON'T DRINK THE WATER—DAVE MATTHEWS BAND VS. THE CHICAGO RIVER

When the Chicago River spat out a raunchy smell in August 2004, **the state of Illinois pointed a finger at the Dave Matthews Band**. No, it wasn't the fact that the annoying guitar-picking single "Satellite" had just been released on yet another live album—the DMB tour bus had just dumped 80 to 100 gallons of "liquid human waste" off a bridge, showering tourists on a boat passing below. The band said they had no memory of the event, but thanks to a truth-telling surveillance video, they were taken to court. Despite their lack of recollection, however, two months later, the band made several $50,000 contributions to environmental groups like Friends of the Chicago River and The Chicago Park District. While the city manned the investigation, owners of Mercury Skyline Yacht Charters filed a suit of their own, claiming that since their passengers had been dumped on (literally and figuratively),

> Chicago city officials canceled a free Smashing Pumpkins concert celebrating the band's tenth anniversary because they feared as many as one hundred thousand people might show up to celebrate. The facility could only hold sixty thousand.

business had gone bad. They wanted damages between $50,000 and $5 million. Luckily for Matthews and band, it was proven that the bus driver, Stefan Wohl, was the only one around when the illegal disposal took place. Generous donations may have gotten DMB off the hook, but Wohl faced criminal charges of reckless conduct and discharging contaminates to pollute the water. He pleaded guilty and took on a few years of probation, community service, and a pretty hefty fine.

★ ★ ★ ★ ★

AN APPLE A DAY—THE BEATLES VS. APPLE COMPUTERS

When The Beatles formed their own recording company to handle their business affairs in the 1960s, they thought they would be original and call the organization Apple Corps. Nearly ten years later, Steve Wozniak and Steve Jobs founded the first Apple computer (and along with it, the multi-million dollar industry Apple Computers). George Harrison didn't think much of the similarity until he spotted a magazine ad for the new fruit on the block and noticed the trademark was remarkably similar to his own. Jobs admitted he had named his company as a "tribute" to the Beatles, and the two mega-companies have been fighting over the copyright ever since. At first, a 1981 agreement outlined that Apple Corps could be the only "Apple" in the world of entertainment, and Apple Computers would stick to the computer industry. However, when Apple Computers launched its iPod and iTunes music store in 2003, they crossed over into the music and entertainment realm. Apple Corps representatives say their rival company breached the contract even further when they began to campaign their new product with the term AppleMusic. The Beatles took them back to court, and Apple Computers settled with them for a cool $27 million. The two Apples seem to have gotten along since then, as John Lennon has been featured in more than one advertisement for the iMac.

> After his death in 2001, Harrison's estate sued his oncologist for pressuring him to sign autographs while ill at home. Dr. Gilbert Lederman was taken to court for showing up at the former Beatles star's home uninvited and using his position as a doctor to obtain "unique collectors' items of enormous value."

★ ★ ★ ★ ★

SUE ME, SUE YOU BLUES—GEORGE HARRISON VS. THE CHIFFONS

The battle between Apple Corps and Apple Computers wasn't George Harrison's only headache in court. A single off his first solo LP in 1970, "My Sweet Lord," became a worldwide hit in no time. Not long after the song's release, however, Harrison was harshly criticized when listeners noticed that a bit of its melody and chords resembled those of The Chiffons' hit "He's So Fine" from just seven years earlier. Bright Tunes, the original publishers of "He's So Fine," took Harrison for a ride in court to the tune of $587,000. Harrison stressed repeatedly that any plagiarism was unintentional.

Subconscious or not, the court sided with The Chiffons, and Harrison had to pay up. Ironically, not long after he settled with his accuser, Beatles' manager Allen Klein purchased the publishing rights to all of Bright Tunes' music.

Three years later, reminiscing on his copyright woes, Harrison made light of his legal problems and entertained supporters with the song "Sue Me, Sue You Blues." He took another stab at Bright Tunes in 1976 when he wrote "This Song," in which he sings "This tune has nothing bright about it." Hoping for the last laugh, Harrison shot a video to promote the new melody set in a courtroom with images of a bailiff hauling him off to jail.

> George Harrison's "My Sweet Lord" made him the first Beatle to have a No. 1 hit after the band's break-up.

★ ★ ★ ★ ★

NOTHING ELSE MATTERS [BUT GETTING OUR NAME OFF GIRLY STUFF]–METALLICA VS. VICTORIA'S SECRET

Heavy metal icons Metallica couldn't stand their kick-ass reputation being associated with panties and lipsticks. In January of 1999, the band noticed that lingerie mogul Victoria's Secret had used its namesake to brand a new shimmering lipstick on their shelves. So they slapped them with a copyright infringement lawsuit stating that they wanted punitive damages and the subsequent halt of all sales of "Metallica" lip pencils. They also requested that any catalogues listing the products be destroyed so as not to confuse bra and makeup shoppers with songs like "Unforgiven." The alleged deception came to an end when the band's attorney settled the suit. The back-to-manly days weren't gone for long, however. Just a few years later, they filed a second lawsuit—this time against a French perfume manufacturer who had released a limited-edition vanilla scent called Metallica.

★ ★ ★ ★ ★

BLAME IT ON THE FAME–MILLI VANILLI VS. EVERYBODY

When **Rob Pilatus and Fab Morvan were denied modeling contracts** in the 1980s, they were so desperate for fame that they decided to put their looks behind a microphone and form the

German hip-hop group Milli Vanilli. The artists could hardly even speak English, but they hoped to use their hard bodies and baby faces to mask the fact that their accents were missing from their music. Milli Vanilli was instantly embraced by pop enthusiasts around the world and was honored as "Best New Artist of the Year" at the 1990 Grammy Awards. After enjoying an ample amount of fame with the singles "Girl You Know It's True" and

THREE THINGS YOU NEVER KNEW ABOUT ... MILLI VANILLI

- The singers whose voices are actually heard on their hit album *Girl You Know It's True* are Johnny Davis, Charles Shaw, and Brad Howell.

- They are the only group to ever have their Grammy Award stripped from them.

- The word "milli" means "national" in Turkish.

"Blame It on the Rain," however, a live performance gone wrong exposed Pilatus and Morvan for the fakes they really were. The tape they were lip-synching to at an MTV concert in Connecticut looped the same line over and over again, and their careers were over in an

After Milli Vanilli was busted for not singing a single lyric on their first album, other artists faced accusations of lip-synching. One of Paula Abdul's former back-up singers claimed the pop diva's voice could rarely be heard on several of the songs on the album *Forever Your Girl*. Mariah Carey was also pressured to schedule a series of live performances to prove that her top-notch notes were not studio tricks but her own.

instant. The band's manager fought for his clients, claiming they weren't doing anything that hadn't been done before. Plenty of producers had taken someone who could barely hum a tune and beefed up vocals with background singers and digital technology. The public didn't buy his ploy.

Although they had sold ten million albums and had three No. 1 hits, fans and radio stations fought back with a class action lawsuit for racketeering and breach of consumer protection laws. The court ruled that anyone who had purchased a Milli Vanilli album could get a refund if they so desired. Desperate for money and the public attention they had long lost, the duo made a Carefree Sugarless Gum commercial in which they poked fun at themselves by lip-synching the jingle. When self-mockery didn't work, they tried actually singing. Insisting that they were, in fact, talented, Pilatus and Morvan tried making music again in 1993 with the self-titled album Rob and Fab, but only three thousand copies were produced. They were never released outside the United States.

★ ★ ★ ★ ★

WHAT MAKES YOU THINK YOU'RE THE ONE (WHO WROTE THAT SONG)- STEVIE NICKS VS. CAROL HINTON

Fleetwood Mac's Stevie Nicks was thrown into a copyright battle when she was sued for allegedly stealing the lyrics to "Sara," one of the most widely played singles from her hit album *Tusk*, released in 1979. Two years after it hit the shelves, the album perked the ears of a stressed-

MOMENT OF STUPIDITY

Back when Eagle Don Henley had a crush on vocalist Stevie Nicks, Mick Fleetwood and John McVie of Fleetwood Mac sent Stevie a bouquet of roses and a note suggesting they get together later that night and put Henley's name on the card. She was so furious at the "offer" that Christine McVie broke the news that it was a prank right away.

out songwriter named Carol Hinton of Rockford, Michigan. Having struggled for years without much success in the music industry, Hinton was furious when she heard "Sara," claiming she had written and submitted the song in a demo tape to Warner Brothers (Fleetwood Mac's recording company) in 1978. She put her accusation against Nicks and her folk-rock band mates on paper, but it simply couldn't hold up in court. Nicks quickly proved that she had sent her own work-in-progress tape of "Sara" to the same recording company in July of 1978, and Hinton's hopes for the credit were crushed.

★ ★ ★ ★ ★

ROCK THE DREIDEL OF LOVE—THE ROCK AND ROLL HALL OF FAME VS. WWW.JEWSROCK.ORG

Journalists David Segal and Jeffery Goldberg and XM Satellite Radio executive Allen Goldberg decided to honor Jewish contributions to rock music with a new website called

the Jewish Rock and Roll Hall of Fame, but the original Cleveland-based Rock Hall flexed its mega-museum muscles and took them to court. Worried that the title would infringe on their trademark, representatives of the original Rock and Roll Hall of Fame and Museum complained that the website had stolen their namesake to simply boost popularity. They also thought the online articles would confuse the public. A former music critic for *The Washington Post*, Segal laughed at the accusation and said he highly doubted an amateur, non-profit website made by "two Jewish guys" would be confused with a museum that has attracted more than 5.5 million tourists since it opened in 1995. The suit was filed regardless, claiming that Cleveland's Rock Hall had "suffered" from the new site (which hadn't even been uploaded to the Internet yet) and wanted damages exceeding $100,000.

In the end, Segal and Goldberg were instructed to remove similar logos and the words "Jewish Rock and Roll Hall of Fame" from their site altogether. Today the website is headlined with the simple title www.JewsRock.org.

★ ★ ★ ★ ★

I SAID I WAS ORIGINAL, BUT I LIED—MICHAEL BOLTON VS. THE ISLEY BROTHERS

Coupled with his long, wavy hair, **Michael Bolton's adult contemporary remakes made him an instant success** when his first single came out in 1991. With a new album of gold nugget R&B hits of the past, it came as a surprise to everyone when Bolton was sued for allegedly ripping off the song "Love Is A Wonderful

Thing" from rock and soul band The Isley Brothers. His fate lay in the hands of a jury, who ruled that he had indeed lifted five elements of the original song. Despite the fact that the two songs in question were remarkably similar in both lyrics and sound, Bolton assured fans that he had never heard another version in his life. He appealed the case to the U.S. Supreme Court, but was denied a second chance. In the end, three representatives had to pay up to compensate for the error—Bolton, Sony Music, and the apparent co-author of Bolton's version of "Love Is A Wonderful Thing." They shelled out a total of $5.4 million, which included much of the profits Bolton had made selling albums with that song on it. However, The Isley Brothers failed to ever make a successful comeback, and by 2000, the band was nearly $5 million in debt.

THREE THINGS YOU NEVER KNEW ABOUT ... MICHAEL BOLTON

- He signed his first record deal at age fifteen, and was belting out power ballads with bar bands long before he was old enough to drink.

- As a child, he idolized R&B greats like Otis Redding, Ray Charles, and Marvin Gaye.

- Since his first album, *Time, Love and Tenderness*, debuted in 1991, Bolton has sold fifty-two million albums and has been awarded six American Music Awards and two Grammy Awards.

★ ★ ★ ★ ★

Come on Baby, Cancel My Tour—The Doors vs. The Doors of the 21st Century

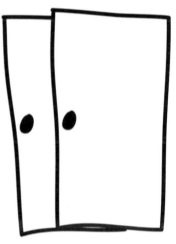

Drummer John Densmore of The Doors was not a happy camper when he found out that guitarist Robby Krieger and keyboardist Ray Manzarek had set out on a new tour without him. He was even more upset when he found out they were playing old favorites under the name The Doors of the 21st Century, marketing their upcoming tour on late-night talk shows as a reunion for hardcore Doors fans from the 1960s. Upset that he (and the late Jim Morrison) had been left out of the deal, Densmore declared that they could call themselves the Hinges, but they could not play under the original band name.

Afraid that The Door's legacy was being flawed by its rebirth as an "oldies act," Densmore teamed up with Jim Morrison's parents and took Krieger and Manzarek to court. A 1971 agreement had outlined that all three surviving band members (along with the

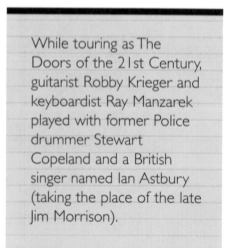

While touring as The Doors of the 21st Century, guitarist Robby Krieger and keyboardist Ray Manzarek played with former Police drummer Stewart Copeland and a British singer named Ian Astbury (taking the place of the late Jim Morrison).

Morrison estate) had to agree on any future use of The Doors name and logo. In the end, the Los Angeles Superior Court ordered that any cash the two non-retired rockers had earned by themselves be shared with Densmore.

★ ★ ★ ★ ★

> Jim Morrison's epitaph is written in Greek. Located in the Cimitière du Père Lachaise in Paris, his gravestone reads James Douglas Morrison, 1943-1971, KATA TON AIMONA EAYTOY, which means, "He did his own thing."

HOW DEEP IS YOUR WALLET FOR ME?—THE BEE GEES VS. RON SELLE

With a slew of songs hitting No. 1 on the Billboard music charts in 1971, **British-Australian pop-turned-funk group The Bee Gees seemed unstoppable**—but their fame and fortune would come into question in 1983, when Chicago antique dealer and songwriter Ron Selle stepped into the picture. Selle accused the band of lifting "How Deep Is Your Love?," made famous by the 1997 best-selling soundtrack for the movie Saturday Night Fever, from his song "Let It End." The song did indeed resemble The Bee Gees' cut-in melody, but that was about it. Regardless, Selle was persistent in his accusations and insisted that he originally recorded the song as a demo from his home, then sent it to a handful of recording companies to consider, none with ties to The Bee Gees, he says. Brothers Barry, Robin, and Maurice Gibb claimed they have always had a policy never to listen to unsolicited songs—and they hardly ever record songs they did not write themselves (with the exception of a few Beatles tunes).

Although Selle's attorneys couldn't prove that the Gibb brothers had ever heard "Let It End," they did manage to convince the jury that the musical bars in the very beginning and the very end of the two songs were strikingly similar. The jury awarded the pitiful lounge singer his damages, but later a sympathetic judge overturned the verdict—Selle simply hadn't proven his case.

★ ★ ★ ★ ★

WHY DON'T YOU BE MY GIRLFRIEND–JUSTIN TIMBERLAKE VS. FIFTEEN-YEAR-OLD FAN

When former 'NSync hottie Justin Timberlake got on his beat box at the group's concerts, he welcomed the endless screams of teenage girls—but

when fifteen-year-old Danielle McGuire smarted off to him after a show that band mate J.C. Chasez was cuter, Timberlake allegedly flipped his lid. In a lawsuit filed by McGuire in December of 2000, the former boyfriend of pop queen Britney Spears was accused of verbally abusing Danielle at a hotel for her smart-aleck comment. Apparently, McGuire and friends had crashed the lobby where the singers were staying, hoping for a handshake or an autograph. When Timberlake walked by without obliging, McGuire shouted out that she didn't care about the snub—she liked J.C. better. After being escorted to an upstairs hallway by a security guard for a few "fighting words" from the singer, McGuire says she was let off the hook when an NBC news affiliate walked in and Timberlake shut his mouth. McGuire, now considering herself a "former" fan, filed suit, but dropped it in 2001 because of heavy publicity.

★ ★ ★ ★ ★

OTHER STARS WHO GOT SUED:

Rap mogul Puff Daddy (or P. Diddy) was doing an interview to promote his tour for the album *Forever* in 1999 when radio deejay Roger Mills asked him the unthinkable—was he involved in the murder of the late rapper Notorious B.I.G.? Diddy's bodyguards retaliated and tried to take the interview tape. Mills allegedly filed suit against Diddy, who was let off the hook by a jury in Detroit.

When punk band Blink 182 first hit the music scene in 1992, they originally called themselves *blink*. After being threatened with a lawsuit from an Irish techno band with the same name, band members Tom Delonge, Mark Hoppus, and Scott Raynor added the 182. Despite rumors that the number represents the number of times actor Al Pacino says the f-word in the movie *Scarface*, the band says the number was chosen at random and means absolutely nothing.

DID YOU KNOW

Travis Barker, who started playing drums when he was four, replaced Scott Raynor in 1998.

Cleveland-based disc jockey Alan Freed pushed urban-blues records on an evening radio show, calling himself the Moondog, and keeping his mic turned on while music played so he could drum out the beat on the table and ad-lib shout-outs such as, "Yeah, daddy! Let's rock and roll!" He even had a theme song that he lifted from a blind New York street musician whose name was also Moondog. Unfortunately, as Freed became more and more famous, the original Moondog threatened to sue, so he changed his show's name to The Rock and Roll Show.

Whitney Houston's father, John, filed a breach of contract lawsuit against her for allegedly not paying him for two years of managing her as an artist. He wanted $100 million but died in February 2003 before settling.

DID YOU KNOW

During the summer of 2005, record industry bigwigs estimated that there were still about 28 billion songs being downloaded illegally every year.

WHAT BIG STARS NAME THEIR BABIES:
IT'S A BOY!

- Brooklyn (Victoria Beckham)
- Diezel Ky and Denim (Toni Braxton)
- Eja (Shania Twain and Mutt Lange)
- Elijah Blue (Cher)
- Maile (Wayne Brady)
- Maison (Rob Thomas)
- Prince (Michael Jackson)
- Rocco (Madonna and Guy Ritchie)
- Romeo (Victoria and David Beckham)
- Seven (Erykah Badu)
- Speck Wildhorse (John Cougar Mellencamp)
- Wolfgang (Eddie Van Halen)
- Zyon (Lauryn Hill)

Chapter 3

Losing My Religion

Losing My Religion

★ ★ ★ ★ ★ ★ ★ ★ ★ ★ ★ ★ ★ ★ ★ ★

Let's face it—being a saint just doesn't sound cool when being a sinner is so much fun. Depravity is what gives most rockers their it-factor, right? You might be surprised. When it comes to being down with religion, some stars hit their knees, some get out their checkbooks, and others simply take a hit of LSD and call their drummer Krishna. Whether they pay their dues to Allah, Jesus, or the devil himself, you might be surprised at the interesting tales of how these artists attempt (yes, attempt) to stick to their faith.

Dee Snider and J.J. French of Twisted Sister, Scott Ian of Anthrax, and Leslie West of Mountain discussed being Jewish and their lives in the music industry on the VH1 special *Matzo and Metal: A Very Classic Passover.*

★ ★ ★ ★ ★

LIKE A PRAYER

Hollywood's self-proclaimed expert on spirituality, Madonna dove headfirst into the Kabbalah, an ancient Jewish mysticism, and has since donated more than $30 million to its headquarters around the world. She has such faith in the religion's sacred book of the law, the Zohar, that she insists it is the foundation for all spiritual beliefs. In fact, in 2004, Madonna gave another $21 million to fund New York's new Kabbalist Grammar School for Children, or K-School, as the kids call it. Regardless of how dedicated the Material Girl is to her belief system, however, most traditional Jewish rabbis would say the mystic way is off base from what The Torah would preach.

Besides the complaints of a few religious leaders, Kabbalah has even more controversy surrounding its New Age push of a special "dynamic living water" to heal body and soul. CultNews.com reported that they had busted the New York

When Madonna and her husband, Guy Ritchie, visited Israel for the Jewish New Year, they spent $2,000 per night shacking up in the largest suite of David's Inter-Continental Hotel.

Center's claims about the product when an unnamed source reported having seen the water bottles being delivered to the center with "product of Canada" stamped on the packaging. Coincidence? Maybe it's blessed beyond the border. On another note, the IRS may even be looking into whether it is an official religion at all, as some reports suggest they are re-evaluating the group's tax-exempt status.

★ ★ ★ ★ ★

RIDIN' THE NOT SO PEACEFUL TRAIN

When Cat Stevens tired of selling forty million albums and paying Great Britain taxes in the mid-70s, he packed up his things and moved to Brazil, where he explored his spirituality like never before. After nearly drowning off the coast of California and begging God to

THREE THINGS YOU NEVER KNEW ABOUT ... KABBALAH

- It teaches that everything in the world is on different levels, and the closer to God you are, the more you can see His godliness.

- It also teaches that the soul is made up of three elements— Nefesh, or the "animal part" everyone gets at birth; Ruach, or the "spirit" of moral virtues; and Neshamah, or the "super-soul" that makes man different from other forms of life.

- Many traditional, organized Jewish groups have complained that the Los Angeles Kabbalah Center popular among celebrities is off base with what they believe to be religious truth.

save him, Stevens committed his life to charity work, joined the Muslim faith, and changed his name to Yusef Islam. He left his former rock legend identity behind, even requesting that the recording industry stop selling his music. They didn't listen.

It wasn't long before government officials suspected Islam was an extremist, and accused him of taking his religious loyalties too far, allegedly supporting the "fatwa" order to kill others in the name of Allah. The former rocker lost his respect among fellow Americans and artists around the globe. In fact, the band 10,000 Maniacs took their remake of his single "Peace Train" off future copies of their albums, and the United States government put his name on a do-not-fly list. While traveling from London to Washington in 2004, Islam's flight was diverted to Maine, and he was detained and deported back to England due to rumors that he was linked to terrorist activities.

At a 1985 Life Aid concert benefiting famine-plagued Ethiopia, Yusef Islam (Cat Stevens) was supposed to make his first live appearance in years singing a song he had written as a tribute for the evening. His performance was cut, however, when the artist before him—Elton John—sang for longer than expected.

★ ★ ★ ★ ★

SLIPPIN' AND A SLIDIN' FOR JESUS

Raised a Seventh-Day Adventist by his parents, Little Richard (Richard Penniman) spent much of his childhood developing his wild gospel roots, and the nonsense babbles and screams of "Tutti Frutti" reveal that he loved to mimic what he saw at church. However, the days of hollerin' for Jesus were over in no time. After proclaiming himself a homosexual and diving into the outlawed abyss of rock and roll, Penniman called it quits as a religious man. His wayward ways as a self-proclaimed sinner wouldn't last long, though. While in Australia for a tour in the 1950s, a scare with a turbulent airplane ride

LITTLE RICHARD

In 1955, Little Richard was recording a demo in New Orleans when he shouted out an off-color, impromptu version of "Tutti Frutti," which was slang for a gay male. Afraid the song would be offensive to just about everyone who heard it, producers changed the lyrics from "Tutti frutti loose booty" to "Tutti frutti all rooty."

changed him for good. When the plane landed, Penniman threw out the flashy jewelry, kissed the ground, and ran back to Jesus. He immediately retired but, true to his form, returned to rock and roll in the 1960s, once he felt he could indeed marry his love for God and music. Since then, Little Richard has worked as a Bible salesman and an evangelist for the Universal Remnant Church of God, where he continues to flip flop between denouncing the demons of secular music and, of course, making secular records.

★ ★ ★ ★ ★

STAIRWAY TO HELL

While he never spit blood onstage like KISS, **Led Zeppelin guitarist Jimmy Page was the ultimate artist of spiritual black magic**. His offstage façade is painted with dark rumors of robes, tarot cards, and even pacts with the devil. In 1970, Page became the proud homeowner of a mansion just off Scotland's Loch Ness. Its appeal? The house faced just the right direction for him to perform specific magic rituals. He even hired a Satanist to paint murals on the walls that would suit his "religious" tastes. In his personal records of his dark practices, Page wrote about how he had summoned so many demons in his day that most of his house help had either gone mad or quit.

> # DID YOU KNOW?
>
> Led Zeppelin's "Stairway to Heaven" was broadcast more than three million times on American airwaves by the end of the 1990s. That adds up to forty-four years of nonstop playtime.

★ ★ ★ ★ ★

GOODBYE BLACK MAGIC WOMAN

Famous for their unique blend of salsa and jazz, Santana flew to the forefront of American rock in the 1970s, but legendary guitarist Carlos felt fatigued by the pressure to maintain a fresh, successful band. Luckily for him, friend (and former guitarist for Miles Davis) John McLaughlin had the answer—a retro-chic following of a Bengalese Hindu philosopher and mystic named Sri Chinmoy. Intrigued by his British pal's dedication to such an interesting theology, Santana jumped on the bandwagon and looked into the faith himself. Later officially converting to the belief system, Santana changed

> Santana's first album hit U.S. charts in 1969 with "Evil Ways," "Jingo," and "Soul Sacrifice."

THREE THINGS YOU NEVER KNEW ABOUT ... SRI CHIMNOY

- At just twelve years old, both of his parents died, and he spent the next twenty years in a "spiritual community" called Sri Aurobindo ashram in India.

- He teaches ultra-fitness, celibacy, and meditation, though many religious leaders worldwide call his following a cult.

- Ashrita Furman, who once held the world record for the most number of world records, told editors at *Hinduism Today* that Sri Chinmoy inspired him to enter a state of transcendence to accomplish feats such as resting a nine-pound brick on his hand for sixty-four miles.

his name to Devadip and recorded his next album, *Love Devotion Surrender*, with McLaughlin in 1974. The new spiritual commitments must have worked because a drug- and stress-free Santana sailed to consistent success all the way up to his Grammy Award-winning *Supernatural* a few years ago.

★ ★ ★ ★ ★

THAT'LL BE THE DAY WHEN I DIE

Known as one of the early influences of the 1950s rock and roll revolution, Buddy Holly may have been known as a religious man, but he certainly

THE EARLY YEARS

Buddy Holly's last name is actually spelled "Holley," but a spelling error in an early contract caused it to be changed in the public eye forever. It wasn't corrected until it was placed on his headstone in 1959.

wasn't restrained by his beliefs. He grew up a young bluegrass musician at Tabernacle Baptist Church in the sleepy hometown of Lubbock, Texas. He made a public profession of faith and was baptized at age fourteen, but barely a teen, the devil wasn't through tempting him yet. At a time when pastors saw rocking and rolling as anything but kin to Jesus Christ, Holly was a religious outlaw. In his

biography, *Buddy Holly*, author Ellis Amburn describes the singer's rebellious days of shoplifting, smoking, drinking, gambling, and "carousing with women." Holly even reportedly told friends that regardless of what he told the churchgoers about having Jesus in his heart, he had little intention of letting go of the sin in his life. According to Amburn, Holly's brother, Larry (who is still a member at Tabernacle Baptist today), believes the Lord took Buddy's life at such a young age because he was too rebellious. Holly died in a plane crash in 1959 at just twenty-three years old.

★ ★ ★ ★ ★

EVERYBODY'S GOT SOMETHING TO HIDE EXCEPT ME AND MY MONK-Y

In the 1960s, eastern spiritual guru Swami Prabhupada was commissioned to evangelize the West with his Hindu know-all and establish the International Society for Krishna Consciousness (ISKCON) in New York City and San Francisco. A fan of "spiritual highs" himself, he related to rock lovers by comparing religious freedoms to being tripped out on LSD, which most Deadheads associated with being close to God (or in fact being God) anyway.

Inspired with a vision for reaching "spiritual" citizens through music, Prabhupada organized a Mantra-Rock Dance concert with acid-rock bands such as the Grateful Dead, Jefferson Airplane, and the Holding Company to raise money to build a temple on the coast. Five thousand people showed up, and Prabhupada welcomed them with an hour-long chant before the music began.

Often referred to as "the quiet one" of The Beatles, George Harrison was obsessed with the music and religious aspects of India. He once abstained from sex because his Hindu guru urged him to... but he ended up having an affair with Ringo Starr's wife, Maureen Cox.

Prabhupada had his hopes set higher than a silly psychedelic rock concert, though. His next goal was to play on the eastern interests of George Harrison and turn The Beatles into walking billboards for the Krishna Conscious cause. Members of ISKCON started sending little messages to the band at their Apple Corps headquarters in London—an apple pie with the Hare Krishna mantra spelled out on top and a record of mantra chantings. When the Fab Four ignored their hints, a devout follower paid Harrison a visit and eventually became his friend. The ploy must have worked because Canadian ISKCON devotees chanted in the background of John Lennon's "Give Peace a Chance." Harrison later took a group from the temple to record a single of the "Hare Krishna Mantra," which became a Top 20 hit in 1969.

★ ★ ★ ★ ★

DANCIN' WITH THE DEVIL

As a boy, Roy Orbison just couldn't get a break when it came to wanting to, as rappers Outkast would say, shake it like a Polaroid picture. As devout members of a Church of Christ congregation in Wink, Texas, Orbison's parents thought dancing was the root of all evil. Naturally, the family had conflicts when Orbison announced that to further the early years of his musical career, he needed to play gigs at local dances. Despite their son's dream to play a few instruments, the Orbisons couldn't bear the thought of Roy giving aid to those sinful rump-bumpers. He resented his parents' pleas, and since he had always felt uncomfortable in the sanctuary, he simply skipped out on Sunday services. Even without Jesus, however, he managed to walk the straight and narrow to some degree—he never struggled with drug or alcohol abuse. In spite of his righteous ways, he would suffer a tragic future. His wife, Claudette, died in a motorcycle accident, and two of his three sons died when the family's Hendersonville, Tennessee, home caught fire in 1968. Orbison's sorrow drove him back to church in the 1970s, and he eventually ended up at a Baptist church with the likes of Johnny Cash and Skeeter Davis.

★ ★ ★ ★ ★

CHURCH-HOUSE ROCK

Ask Reverend James E. Hamill of Memphis, Tennessee, how pretty Elvis's voice was in the choir, and he will quickly debunk the myth—though Elvis attended with his parents for several years, Presley never sang in his church once. In fact, he never even became an official member of the church. In the late 1950s, Presley sought redemption with the old pastor and visited him after one Sunday evening service to talk about his misery. Hamill, who wasn't very happy that anyone who used to hear his preaching could ever lead a life of such sinful "entertaining," listened to him moan about how his money, his fame, and his rebellion had brought him no joy.

Near the end of his life while performing in Las Vegas several years later, Presley asked again whether he should turn his talents back to God—he met with evangelist Rex Humbard and talked to him about whether he should quit the rock scene and start singing only gospel music. Humbard said no.

fabulous firsts

Elvis Presley made his first appearance on national television singing "Blue Suede Shoes" and "Heartbreak Hotel" on The Dorsey Brothers Show in 1956.

★ ★ ★ ★ ★

SMOKE GANJA, NO CRY

Dating back to the 1914 founding of the Universal Negro Improvement and Conservation Association, Rastafari was key to the rapid-spreading rumor that Ethiopia was the supreme and black people were superior to all others. After the "Negro Bible" came out, insisting that the God and all of his messengers described in Christian Scriptures were

69

dark-skinned, the Rastafari dream caught the ears of Bob Marley. The official founder of the religion, Leonard Howell, spread the word that eventually all blacks who were exiled from their "homeland" would one day return. Marley liked what he heard and put the message to a rockin' reggae beat to let the world know it wasn't just the Caribbean that supported this new belief system.

> Bob Marley grew up in a Pentecostal church that incorporated African pagan traditions of chanting, dancing, and warding off evil with "good" magic. The family had hoped he would become a white witch like his grandfather—but instead he chose music.

Using reggae as a way to socially respond to the poverty around him, Marley sold more than $250 million worth of records and was considered by his religion as a prophet and a priest. He found some inspiration in the Bible, relating to the Psalms and the plight of the Old Testament Israelites who were living in captivity. Rastafari's most well known practice of escaping captivity and creating harmony among the peoples is smokin' the ganja, a "spiritual herb" used to purify the soul and reveal wickedness. Marley and friends believed the devil hated ganja and that certain verses in Genesis supported it, such as Genesis 1:29 (KJV), which reads, "Behold, I have given you every herb bearing seed."

MOMENTS OF STUPIDITY

In 1968, Neil Diamond supported a new organization called Performers Against Drugs and even wrote a song, "The Pot Smoker's Song," that included testimonials of former drug addicts. Less than ten years later, he was arrested for possession of marijuana.

★ ★ ★ ★ ★

MxPx

While most Christian bands assign themselves obvious names of faith, such as Point of Grace and Casting Crowns, religious rockers MxPx have no such pretense. In fact, the name of their band is an inside joke between friends, poking fun at someone's "magnification plaid" shirt. They don't play in sanctuaries. In fact, they don't play in churches at all. Lead singer Mike Herrera says his band has never been out to preach—they just want to play good music. But they do pray before shows and take opportunities to influence other punk bands on the music scene.

Not long after MxPx went mainstream, other rockers were asking the band questions about the Bible and asking them to pray for their families. Hoping to change the pretense that Christianity is a weird minority, MxPx isn't afraid to announce their beliefs when asked. In all, the band just sticks to their punk sound and lets the lyrics do the witnessing. In "Party, My House, Be There," the band purposefully leaves out the usual punk references to drug and alcohol use. In "Tomorrow's Another Day," they sing about how God is faithful even when hope is lost.

★ ★ ★ ★ ★

OTHER ARTISTS OF FAITH:

- Rapper Kanye West paid $350,000 to have a painter recreate the Sistine Chapel ceiling in his home.

- The lead singer of Disturbed grew up in an Orthodox Jewish family and almost became a rabbi.

- Black Sabbath's Ozzy Osbourne got his start playing R&B in a church basement.

- Alice Cooper once claimed to be born-again, but after hearing the rumor that he ripped the head off a live chicken at a concert, clergymen beg to differ.

- As a child, Michael Jackson went door-to-door as a missionary, passing out copies of *Watchtower* magazine.

- Phish sometimes performs a version of the High Holiday prayer in Hebrew.

- Prince was born into a Seventh-Day Adventist family, but later converted to Jehovah's Witness.

★ ★ ★ ★ ★

ROCKERS' WACKY THOUGHTS ON RELIGION

- "My experience of God came from acid. It's the most important thing that ever happened to me." —Brian Wilson, the Beach Boys

- "God isn't a pill, but LSD explained the mystery of life. It was a religious experience." —Paul McCartney

- "As God has been losing his percentage, the devil has been picking up." —John Phillips, the Mamas and the Papas

- "There are black musicians who think we are acting as unknown agents of Lucifer and others who think we are Lucifer. Everybody's Lucifer." —Keith Richards, the Rolling Stones

- "I feel so close to the Lord when I'm that aroused. Never closer." —Prince

DID YOU KNOW

"Joy To the World" by Three Dog Night was originally written by Hoyt Axton for a new animated children's television show (*The Happy Song*) that was never produced nor aired.

Chapter 4

Controversial Moments in Rock History

Controversial Moments in Rock History

★ ★ ★ ★ ★ ★ ★ ★ ★ ★ ★ ★ ★ ★ ★ ★

Think of the word "scandal," and one of two arenas probably come to mind: politics and sports. But what about celebrities in the music industry? With loads of cash and something to prove to competitors, most rock stars are itching to make their opinions known through controversial songs and music videos. From the very first time Elvis swung his hips on live television, to the shocking moment when **AC/DC** realized their band name was gay, America has loved every minute. Scandals sell, and if it has to be through wild reputations, cheesy band lyrics, shady business deals, or ridiculous racial tensions, some stars say, "So be it."

Drummer Keith Moon was involved in an accident that left his driver, Neil Boland, dead. Moon was invited to a disco opening in Hatfield, but the scene was not what he thought it would be. Boland was trying to drive away when a group of young people began attacking their car. Boland got out of the Bentley, trying to protect it, but the car continued to roll forward. Moon and another passenger tried to stop it, grabbing the wheel, but were unsuccessful. Boland was run over and killed.

★ ★ ★ ★ ★

(HE) SHOOK ME ALL NIGHT LONG (MOST CONTROVERSIAL BAND TITLE)

When Angus and Malcolm Young first formed their power-chord group AC/DC at just fourteen and nineteen years old (respectively), it was initially just an innocent ploy to spite their brother, who had just joined a successful new band himself. However, when it came to beating their rivals with a rockin' band name, the Young Brothers flopped. They were psyched when they came up with AC/DC, an acronym they had read off the front of a sewing machine, but they didn't quite catch on to the fact that it suggested something a little more than electric currents—in some parts of the country, AC/DC was slang for being bisexual. A few awkward moments later (*and* after dodging the rumor that their name stood for "Anti-Christ Devil's Children"), the band decided to make the most of a queer situation and make some money off their slip-up. Just starting out and desperate for gigs, they were hired to play at a handful of gay clubs and parties.

> ### YOUNG AND DUMB
>
> AC/DC front man Angus Young was a little confused when it came to fashion. First, he wore a gorilla suit on stage. When that didn't elicit just the right rocker façade, he tried a Zorro outfit. Nope, still not outrageous enough. In one last attempt to be original, Young tried an Australian schoolboy get-up recommended by his sister. It stuck.

★ ★ ★ ★ ★

DON'T STAND SO CLOSE TO ME (MOST CONTROVERSIAL CLASH OF BAND MEMBERS)

Drummer Stewart Copeland may have been the glue that initially bound and sustained The Police through its early days, but when Sting came along, the newbie became the poster child for everything pop. A jealous Copeland turned sour, and the two international stars quickly became known for their prideful clashes when one seemed to have more groupies than the other. The two fame-hungry stars were rumored to be at each other's throats at all times. When Sting would write a hit, Copeland would rewrite it as his own. When Copeland would get the band together for a recording session, Sting would get him his own "private" studio to keep him out of the way.

> The Police released their first single, "Fall Out," in February 1977.

★ ★ ★ ★ ★

STRANGE FRUIT (MOST CONTROVERSIAL SONG)

At the fragile beginning of the Civil Rights Movement in the late 1930s, Jewish poet, schoolteacher, and passionate Communist Abel Meeropol caught a gruesome glimpse of a photograph that changed his life forever. A candid shot of a black man being lynched in the racist South, the photo disturbed him to such an extent that he took on a pen name (Lewis Allan) and wrote the emotional poem "Strange Fruit." His words were candid and descriptive with the lines "Southern trees bear a strange fruit / Blood on the leaves and blood at the root / Black body swinging in the southern breeze / Strange fruit hanging from the poplar trees." The honesty of the poem caught the ears and heart of a twenty-four-year-old Billie Holiday, who begged her recording company to let her remake it to music. When denied, she went to another label and finally released the tune in 1939. However, her persistence nearly led to her downfall as an artist. Civil rights activists quickly adopted "Strange Fruit" as an inspirational anthem, and Holiday's white fans were disappointed in her social and political outspokenness. When she performed the song onstage, she suffered verbal and sometimes physical abuse at the hands of her own admirers. Radio stations refused to play it, and *Time* magazine called it nothing more than propaganda. "Strange Fruit" practically disappeared from airwaves until a U.S. congressman got hold of a copy and spread it across the nation as a statement against Southerners' brutal treatment of blacks.

CELEBRITY ALIAS

Alias: Billie Holiday
Actual Name: Eleanora Fagan

★ ★ ★ ★ ★

I Just Called To Say I'm Sorry (Most Controversial Apologies)

When it comes to blurting out the unthinkable (and subsequently having to put a foot in their mouths), many rock stars have spouted off comments or gestures to fans and journalists they wish they could take back. All convictions (and bad habits) aside, these rockers had to bite their lips and say they were sorry, whether they meant it or not.

John Lennon—John Lennon's lyrics in songs like "God" and "Imagine" revealed to fans that he often struggled with questions about religion. It may have been acceptable to explore his questions in song, but when he told a reporter at the *London Evening Standard* that Christianity would eventually disappear and that The Beatles were "more popular than Jesus" in 1966, he had to apologize to praying people around the world. While Londoners seemed to have no problem with Lennon's metaphor,

LENNON

Americans were furious and burnt their albums in protest when the interview was reprinted in the teenybopper magazine *DATEbook*. The artist wasn't very happy about having to apologize for what he said was a quote taken out of context. Regardless, conservative parents everywhere finally had the confirmation they needed to label the longhaired Fab Four as nothing more than the epitome of rock and roll evil.

David Bowie—Controversy came knocking on David Bowie's door when he gave the Nazi salute to people cheering at him in public. Combined with his comments in a *Playboy* magazine interview suggesting Hitler was respectable and Great Britain could "benefit from a fascist leader," Bowie didn't impress fans much. Later, he humbled himself and admitted he had probably shot off the phrase in the middle of a cocaine high. Bowie left the country in shame and made his new home in Berlin.

Janet Jackson—The term "wardrobe malfunction" took on a whole new meaning when, thanks to the sticky hands of 'NSync dreamboat Justin Timberlake, Janet Jackson flashed a breast to 140 million people watching the live Super Bowl halftime show in 2004. Despite the fact that an MTV posting the week before the game read "Janet Jackson's Super Bowl show promises shocking moments," Jackson claims the channel knew nothing about the last-minute plan for Timberlake to rip off a piece of her corset. The Monday immediately after the event, the Federal Communications Commission issued an investigation, and CBS ended up with a record-breaking $550,000 fine—the largest fine ever issued to a television broadcaster.

Bono—While partying with California rockers The Red Hot Chili Peppers in the Dublin Clarence Hotel, U2 front man Bono was caught lighting up a cigarette and violating Ireland's new

CELEBRITY ALIAS

Alias: Bono
Actual Name: Paul Hewson

ban on smoking. After staff and friends reminded him of the new law, he put it out and penned a formal apology to the country's outraged health fanatics. The ironic thing—Bono co-owns the Clarence Hotel with his band mates.

★ ★ ★ ★ ★

THE ART OF [APPARENT] SELF-DESTRUCTION (MOST CONTROVERSIAL MUSIC VIDEO)

When industrial rock group Nine Inch Nails was brainstorming for cool effects to put in their new music video for the song "Down In It," they thought it would be

pretty awesome if lead vocalist and keyboarder Trent Reznor were portrayed as dead. After a heavy dose of pale makeup, Reznor lay on the ground while his band mates tied the camera to a helium balloon for a cool angle shot from above. However, the balloon-cam drifted away and landed in a nearby field. NIN never recovered the video, but the farmer who found it was so freaked out that he gave the tape to the Federal Bureau of Investigation.

★ ★ ★ ★ ★

TALK THIS WAY (MOST CONTROVERSIAL LYRICS)

In 1963, one of the most famous rock songs of all time, "Louie Louie," caused a panic among parents and preachers looking to keep their teenagers pure when it was initially thought to be the most filthy song to ever hit the airwaves. Rumors of its unthinkable (and incomprehensible) lyrics quickly spread to Washington, D.C., and the FBI stepped in to examine whether the song violated federal obscenity laws or was simply one of the dumbest, most meaningless pieces ever written. The investigation, which lasted nearly three years, concluded that there was

DID YOU KNOW
With the exception of Paul McCartney's "Yesterday," "Louie Louie" has been covered more times than any other pop song.

no "dirty" version of "Louie Louie" floating through the radio frequencies. In fact, some say the only reason the lyrics turned out so dang hard to understand was that lead singer Jack Ely was hoarse from singing a ninety-minute jam session the night before (not to mention the fact that he was wearing braces). Others say the studio's boom microphone wasn't set up correctly. Regardless, the day he recorded the new song, Ely had no idea that he was actually working on the final cut—he simply thought it was a rehearsal. In the end, the band liked what they heard and decided to keep it—mumbles and all.

★ ★ ★ ★ ★

I Stole Your Lyrics (Most Controversial Plagiarism)

Fire-breathing vocalist and bassist Gene Simmons and guitarist Paul Stanley wrote the line "The bigger the cushion, the better the pushin'" in the single "Spit," from their 1992 album *Revenge*. However clever the metaphor seemed at the time, though, fans were quick to notice that the lyrics were almost identical to a song by rival rockers Spinal Tap called "Big Bottom," which read "the bigger the cushion, the sweeter the pushin'." Simmons and Stanley claimed that in spite of any apparent copycat conundrum, they had

THREE THINGS YOU NEVER KNEW ABOUT... KISS

- Ever the master thespian, Gene Simmons made a cameo in the little-known film *Red Surf* in 1990.
- The band's first big gig was at The Coventry in Queens, New York.
- "God Gave Rock 'N' Roll to You II" was originally recorded by Argent, a group who once opened for KISS, for the film soundtrack of *Bill & Ted's Bogus Journey*.

never even heard of Spinal Tap and therefore could never have plagiarized the line.

★ ★ ★ ★ ★

UNDER THE TABLE AND DEALING (MOST CONTROVERSIAL DISC JOCKEY)

GUITARIST WHO ROCKS

Ace Frehley

Band: Kiss

Guitar of Choice: Gibson Les Paul

Best Known For: "Shock Me" on the album *Love Gun*

Broadcast live from New York at the height of its popularity in the late 1950s, *American Bandstand* had twenty million fans and was being carried on at least sixty-four television stations. However, some music industry veterans were suspicious of how selective host Dick Clark was when it came to choosing bands to showcase on the air. He seemed to give artists represented by Philadelphia recording companies more airtime than the rest. Clark also owned partial copyrights to 150 songs and was accused of playing those specific songs over and over again to boost record sales and, in turn, his own profits. In the end, a 1959 U.S. Senate committee investigated the case, and Clark admitted to one of the allegations—he had accepted a lavish gift (a fur stole and some jewelry) from the president of a well-known recording company. Other than that, investigators could not find anything worth trying him for, so Clark agreed to behave and give up the extracurricular business deals to focus on *Bandstand* instead.

> B.B. King is the only performer who did *not* lip-synch on *American Bandstand.*

★ ★ ★ ★ ★

THE HIGH COST OF LOW LIVIN' (MOST CONTROVERSIAL FAN)

The Allman Brothers made a name for themselves when they blended smooth southern soul with psychedelic rock and country in the 1970s, but with a drug-induced wild side, their concerts sometimes got a little out of control. A roadie with a passion for rock, Twiggs Lyndon did not appreciate it when a Buffalo, New York, club owner refused to pay The Allman Brothers for their performance because they showed up late. Standing up for his favorite band and venting his frustration, Lyndon whipped out a fishing knife and stabbed the owner multiple times. Shocked at what its self-proclaimed No. 1 fan had just done, the band returned to its tour and let the cops take care of Lyndon, who was arrested for first-degree murder.

Lyndon's defense in trial seemed ridiculous at first—he claimed to have been temporarily insane from

> ## THE EARLY YEARS
> Duane and Gregg Allman played in a band called the Allman Joys before forming the Allman Brothers Band in 1969.

spending too much time on the road with The Allman Brothers. In the end, his assertion was not as unbelievable as it initially sounded. When drummer Berry Oakley was called to testify, he spent so much time running back and forth to throw up in the bathroom that everyone began to wonder if Lyndon's insanity ploy was actually true. The dominance drugs had over Oakley (and his bandmates) became so obvious that Lyndon was found not guilty.

★ ★ ★ ★ ★

Ashes to Ashes (Most Controversial Deaths)

Rolling Stone Rocker Brian Jones: On July 2, 1969, Brian Jones was found dead in the swimming pool at his home. While the

coroner suggested he had drowned while swimming under the influence of drugs and alcohol, his friends and family have disputed the theory for the last thirty-five years. His girlfriend, Anna, even wrote a book about the incident, titled *The Murder of Brian Jones*, which claimed that Jones had not drowned on his own but that someone had held his head underwater until he lost consciousness.

Seattle Grunge Gal Mia Zapata: A twenty-seven-year-old up-and-coming star of the Seattle grunge band the Gits, Mia Zapata was last seen alive hanging out with friends at her favorite bar. A few hours later, her father got a call from the coroner asking him to come and identify her body, which had been found on the side of the road. With their victim being so young and so locally famous, police felt pressure to solve the case—but it took more than a decade to even match DNA found on her body to a Cuban-born fisherman who was living in the Florida Keys. He was sentenced to thirty-seven years in prison.

R&B Diva Aaliyah: On August 25, 2001, twenty-two-year-old Aaliyah was flying to Miami from a trip to the Bahamas when her plane, weighed down with too much luggage (and the singer's beefy bodyguards), crashed into a marsh just after lift off. Her pilot had allegedly been convicted of possessing crack cocaine just weeks before and was not even licensed to fly in those skies.

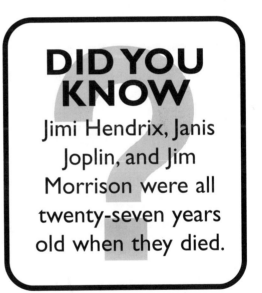

DID YOU KNOW?

Jimi Hendrix, Janis Joplin, and Jim Morrison were all twenty-seven years old when they died.

Chicago Lead Guitarist Terry Kath: On January 23, 1978, Terry Kath was cleaning his guns at a party in his home when a friend told him to put them away before somebody got hurt. Joking that there weren't even bullets in the barrels, Kath put one to his head and pulled the trigger. He was killed instantly.

★ ★ ★ ★ ★

Taboo Tunes (Most Controversial Censorship)

After the ashes fell and New York began cleaning up Ground Zero in the fall of 2001, Americans were a little hesitant when it came to any potential signs of future terrorist attacks on U.S. soil. The emotional aftermath of those grieving lost loved ones even led executives at Clear Channel Communications to reevaluate what was playing on their airwaves. Were there songs insensitive to the families affected or suggestive of celebrating such a tragic day? In turn, Clear Channel made a controversial move that would upset some listeners and comfort others—the company temporarily blacklisted songs with "questionable lyrics" from their stations' play lists. The tunes frowned upon included:

- AC/DC—"Highway to Hell"

- The Bangles—"Walk Like an Egyptian"

- Beastie Boys—"Sabotage"

- Dave Matthews Band—"Crash into Me"

- Led Zeppelin—"Stairway to Heaven"

- Red Hot Chili Peppers—"Aeroplane"

- U2—"Sunday Bloody Sunday"

- Queen—"Another One Bites the Dust"

- Foo Fighters—"Learn to Fly"

- Cat Stevens—"Morning Has Broken"

- Black Sabbath—"War Pigs"

- Paul McCartney and Wings—"Live And Let Die"

- Simon and Garfunkel—"Bridge Over Troubled Water"

★ ★ ★ ★ ★

CONCERTS GONE WRONG (MOST CONTROVERSIAL CONCERTS)

Thanks to the thousands of concerts of old, all rockers know that mosh pits plus alcohol (plus pyrotechnics) equals serious problems. But unfortunately for these Deadheads, they didn't listen and paid the price as they hosted the most controversial concerts in history.

At a 1969 Altamont rock concert in northern California, featuring The Rolling Stones, Jefferson Airplane, and The Grateful Dead, eighteen-year-old Meredith Hunter was parting with friends when she was allegedly beaten and stabbed to death by the security, Hell's Angels. Three other people were also reported to have died at the concert—two from a hit-and-run accident and another from an alleged drowning in a drainage ditch. The violence of the drug-induced rioting crowds became so bad that many of the bands refused to take stage.

At a 1970s show featuring Frank Zappa and The Mothers of Invention at the Montreux Casino in Switzerland, one idiotic fan

91

fired a flare gun at the ceiling and burnt the place to the ground. The band Deep Purple memorialized both the casino and the accident when they sang about it in the song "Smoke on the Water," which included the lyrics, "Frank Zappa & the Mothers were at the best place around / But some stupid with a flare gun burned the place to the ground / Smoke on the water, fire in the sky." The casino was rebuilt, and reopened in 1975.

In a poor attempt to emulate the historical success of the first Woodstock Festival in 1969, MTV hosted the infamous Woodstock 1999 in upstate New York. Attended by more than two hundred thousand people, the event was plagued with violence, riots, and reports of rape allegations. At least five hundred policemen had been hired as security, and a twelve-foot fence made of wood and steel was built to keep out the inevitable party crashers, but in the end the fence came down, ATMs were broken into, and vendor booths were set on fire. MTV pulled its crews out quickly. All they could do was watch the angry mob destroy the place.

In 2003, a whopping ninety-seven people died in a Rhode Island nightclub called The Station, where rockers Great White were performing. The club manager said he had no idea the band would be bringing fireworks, and a pyrotechnics error set the place on fire, trapping many concert-goers inside a blazing inferno. Because the building was built before 1979, it did not have a sprinkler system, which firefighters said would have put out the fire immediately. It burnt to the ground.

DIE HARD FANS DO THE DUMBEST THINGS

- The President of the Worldwide Elvis Fan Club, Henry Newinn of Houston, Texas, once announced that he had discovered a patch of bark on a tree with a striking resemblance to the King's profile. The tree was in his own backyard.

- When six hundred thousand people crowded to hear the Allman Brothers play in New York in 1973, one super fan decided to make a grand entrance with fireworks and a parachute. As he jumped out of the plane, he lit and threw a stick of dynamite into the air, forgetting that it would fall at the same rate as he. The dynamite exploded mid-air and killed him before he ever reached the ground.

- Bob Dylan once noticed one of his most enthusiastic (and most nosy) neighborhood fans, A.J. Weberman, regularly nosed through his garbage for scraps of poetry and personal items. Dylan got so upset that he met Weberman on a New York City street and beat him up.

★ ★ ★ ★ ★

SAY IT LOUD—I'M BLACK AND I'M PROUD (MOST CONTROVERSIAL RACISTS)

During the 1940s, rock and roll was just taking root across America as a rebellious teenage phenomenon. Parents weren't happy with the sexual references in the new songs popping up across the charts or with the term "rock and roll" itself, which traditionally referred to sex in popular blues tunes. To try and skirt the negative connotations associated with rhythm and blues, major recording companies fueling album sales and recruiting new stars decided to abandon black artists and audiences altogether. Their talent scouts were predominately white and had such little knowledge of black tastes that they often completely overlooked the demographic. Most admitted that they felt that blacks had such a sparse income that they would never buy enough records to influence the music industry anyway. Overall, racial bias ruled the airwaves—with the exception of a few catchy tunes by Nat King Cole, The Mills Brothers, and The Ink Spots, which were in high demand by white audiences. In the end, smaller independent music companies popped up around the country to fill in the void and push talented black artists back to the top of mainstream music: Atlantic Records of New York, Chess Records of Chicago, King Records of Cincinnati, Specialty Records of Los Angeles, and Sun Records of Memphis.

★ ★ ★ ★ ★

COLOR ME BAD (MOST CONTROVERSIAL ANTI-RACIST)

Famous for coining the term "rock and roll," **popular disc jockey Alan Freed carried his fame into the world of television** in 1957 with a show not too different from *American Bandstand*. A self-proclaimed "racially color-blind" host, he had no problem showing white and black teens sharing the stage. But when African-American Frankie Lymon of the band Teenagers danced on air with a white woman, viewers were outraged that Freed would dare to promote such racial tolerance. Southern affiliates could not ignore the uproar and shut down the show.

Freed moved on to broadcast locally, sticking to a more open-minded New York crowd, but the racial tension wasn't over yet. Now it was the black community's turn to take a punch at his impartiality. Why, they asked, should a white producer make so much money off the success of talented black artists? When Freed's bosses at his radio station, WIN, heard rumors of controversy, they didn't have enough public relations propaganda to defend themselves and simply let the issue lie. The turmoil continued, however, and riots broke out at local concerts Freed organized. To prevent continued trouble the following year, WIN chose not to renew his contract.

In the end, however, it would be financial woes rather than racial strain that would end Freed's career. On March 15, 1964, he was indicted by a federal grand jury for alleged tax evasion, claiming he had never paid the IRS taxes on a large sum of his income. He may have been living in Palm Springs, California, but he was no aristocrat. Freed was poor, out of a job, and being pressured to shell out more

> Crossing his fingers for a good turnout, disc jockey Alan Freed once rented out a facility that could hold ten thousand for his Moondog Coronation Ball in 1952. He underestimated, though, and twenty thousand people showed up. Due to overcrowding, the show had to be canceled, but Freed went on to plan other events that would have an attendance of up to one hundred thousand.

than $30,000 to the U.S. government. He fell ill and died at age forty-three before he could even think about coming up with the cash.

MO' MONEY, MO' PROBLEMS (MOST CONTROVERSIAL MONEY-MAKING SCHEME)

Long before Napster and iTunes, the American Society of Composers and Publishers (ASCAP) found a tricky way to make as much money as possible off radio producers on the cutting edge of new technologies.  With complete ownership over the artists whose songs were appearing on air for the first time, they charged radio stations to rent sheet music, band programs, and variety shows to fill up the airtime in each market. They also charged stations for each time they featured one of its artists. The ASCAP made a fortune, but producers thought the policy was crap and soon rebelled, arguing that they should not have to pay for the music. Each time a song played was free advertising for the artist, wasn't it? It generated album sales, didn't it? Disc jockeys had the power to make or break an artist's career based on how many times they played a song on the air, so they took their power to the bank and formed Broadcast Music Incorporated (BMI) to skirt the sky-high fees. New artists caught on to the free publicity and the demand for the BMI genius went through the roof.

★ ★ ★ ★ ★

WHO IS THE FIFTH BEATLE? (MOST CONTROVERSIAL CLAIM)

Over the years, many Beatles fans have tried to put a finger on which fifth wheel associated with the Fab Four has the right to be called the fifth and final Beatle. While many groupies, managers, and buddies came and went throughout the years, only these guys make the running. Who will it be? You be the judge.

Pete Best—A drummer for the Beatles from August 1960 to August 1962, Best played with the Fab Four during their famous tour

DID YOU KNOW

Even though they broke up twenty-five years ago, The Beatles continue to sell more records each year than the Rolling Stones.

of Germany and on the renowned *Anthology I* collection. With a little help from his mommy, who bragged on her son's new endeavor, the band slowly became famous. However, Best's band mates admitted he wasn't the greatest drummer they had ever heard. When the longhaired boys signed their first record deal, producer George Martin broke the news

that he wanted to replace Best with someone, well, better. Ringo Starr stepped in, but fans weren't comfortable with him right away. At first the Beatles were harassed at concerts by Best fans who missed their old friend. Best's career would never quite recover. He spent the rest of the sixties poor and bouncing between B-list bands before he retired to work at a bakery and later as a civil servant in Liverpool.

> ### CELEBRITY ALIAS
> Alias: Ringo Starr
> Actual Name: Richard Starkey

Brian Epstein—The Beatles' manager from 1961-1967, Epstein was a theater student and a manager at a family-owned North End Music Store when he first met the band while chillin' at a nightclub. He had never managed before, but he went nuts when he heard the Beatles perform at Liverpool's Cavern Club in 1961 and promised he could make them superstars. Ever the fashion guru, it was Epstein who gave the Fab Four their matching suits and haircuts, and in less than six months, he had gotten them a recording contract. His loyalty to The Beatles didn't go unnoticed by his other clients, though. They regularly complained of not getting the marketing they deserved as they took a backseat to Epstein's "Yesterday" pretty boy project.

George Martin—A bigwig at Parlophone Records, Martin was the producer of most Beatles albums, including the original recording of "Let It Be." He was the first to let the band experiment with their sound and write their own music. Even when Martin's instincts told him the guys should stick to work from outside writers, he let them try some original songs and overdubs that helped mold their sound. Hungry for a bigger paycheck, Martin was denied a raise and quit Parlophone in 1965 to form his own company but continued to work with The Beatles. Even after the band broke up, he produced records for Ringo Starr and Paul McCartney. Since then, he has worked with the likes of industry veterans Celine Dion and Elton John.

Neil Aspinall—A classic fifth wheel who befriended the band while renting a room in Pete Best's house, Aspinall became The Beatles' road manager. He had originally considered going to school to be an accountant but soon found his alternate calling driving the band back and forth from gigs. He ditched the college dream and decided to stick around. When his drummer roomie was fired in 1962, Aspinall had plans to quit the project ... but Best told him not to be stupid. It was a good move because he ended up doing an array of odd jobs for the band, and was even invited to play instruments on the original recordings of "Within You Without You" and "Being Mr. Kite." Later, he became the managing director of Apple Corps, The Beatles' personal record company.

Mal Evans—An engineer in Liverpool, Evans spent a lot of free time at the Cavern Club and eventually earned enough respect to be hired on as a bouncer. While he was throwing out the drunks and breaking up bar fights, Evans befriended The Beatles and their manager, Brian Epstein. He was a charmer and eventually was brought on as a roadie to help set up the equipment at gig sites.

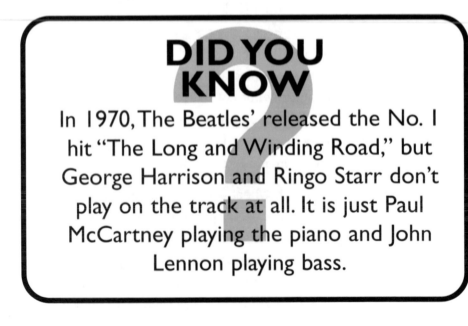

DID YOU KNOW

In 1970, The Beatles' released the No. 1 hit "The Long and Winding Road," but George Harrison and Ringo Starr don't play on the track at all. It is just Paul McCartney playing the piano and John Lennon playing bass.

Chapter 5

Papa's Got a Brand New Bag: How Big Stars Blow Their Dough

Papa's Got a Brand New Bag: How Big Stars Blow Their Dough

★ ★ ★ ★ ★ ★ ★ ★ ★ ★ ★ ★ ★ ★ ★ ★

I n their younger days, money didn't come so easy to the filthy rich stars of today. Madonna worked behind the counter at Dunkin' Donuts. David Lee Roth changed bedpans and bed sheets as a hospital orderly. Vince Neil was an electrician, Rod Stewart was a gravedigger, and Jon Bon Jovi flipped hamburger patties at Burger King. These rockers may have searched their car for quarters years ago, but these days they follow the golden rule of riches—if you've got it, flaunt it.

> In 1999, Mariah Carey bought Marilyn Monroe's white baby grand piano for $662,500.

★ ★ ★ ★ ★

RUBY TUESDAY

When it comes to showing off their hard-earned bread, no one does it like rappers. But long before *their* platinum grills hit the red carpet, **Mick Jagger of The Rolling Stones flashed his cash when he implanted an emerald into one of his teeth** on the upper right side of his mouth. Unfortunately, from a distance it looked more like a bit of broccoli than a precious jewel. When friends kept telling him he had food in his teeth, Jagger swapped it for a ruby. When they started handing him tissues to wipe the spot of "blood" off his mouth, he learned that red, too, wasn't quite his color. Refusing to give up so easy on something so dang cool, he swapped once more—this time for a diamond.

★ ★ ★ ★ ★

DON'T STOP SPENDING TIL YOU GET ENOUGH

Dropping dollars on jewelry and expensive toys is a signature pastime of rockers worldwide, but nothing compares to how they blow millions to shine on MTV and VH1. Hoping to shock viewers (and sell more records) with state-of-the-art special effects, producers will break the bank when it comes to constructing the hottest music videos of all time. And no one does it like pop king Michael Jackson. In 1983, the groundbreaking thirteen-minute "Thriller" was the most expensive music video ever made at $1 million (which translates to nearly double that amount today). However, Jackson has since one-upped

> The longest amount of time it ever took Elton John to write a song was three-and-a-half hours for "Paris." In an interview with a reporter from CNN, he said that the duration drove him nuts and that he thought he was going to have a "mental breakdown."

himself with the video for "Scream," a futuristic duo with sister Janet Jackson that cost a jaw-dropping $7 million. The pair spent at least $11,000 a day on makeup alone. Was it worth the big bucks? Also boasting the theme song for kiddie flick *Free Willy 2*, Jackson's album at the time, *HIStory*, only sold 3.5 million copies.

★ ★ ★ ★ ★

LUCY IN THE SKY WITH ALBUMS

What kind of morning shopping ritual would a colorful male diva sporting thousands of pairs of designer glasses and fifteen hit singles have? Every Tuesday morning at 9:30 a.m., Elton John swings by Tower Records in Atlanta, Georgia, to flip through new album releases. Because he's, well, Elton John, employees let him slip in before the store opens to sip coffee and take a gander at hundreds of CDs alphabetized on carts waiting to be distributed throughout the store. Elton simply buys the ones he wants and sneaks out before the store is packed with shoppers.

★ ★ ★ ★ ★

EXPRESS YOURSELF (WITH INK)

Taboo in many parts of the world, tattoos have been the ultimate (and most permanent) means of self-expression since prehistoric times. In East Asian countries, most people with body art keep it covered because tattoos are so closely associated with criminal activity. In Japan, businesses and recreational facilities ban those with visible tatoos. It's this outlaw image that

OOPS ... I DID IT AGAIN

When Britney Spears had a Hebrew tattoo put on the back of her neck in 2004, she thought it stood for "new era," in honor of her dedication to Kabbalah. However, Spears had two things wrong—the symbol actually stood for "protection," and she failed to realize that in Judaism, the very act of getting a tattoo is a sinful taboo. What makes the situation even more ironic is that it was not the first time she was duped by a tattoo artist. In 2003, a friend told her that the tattoo on her hip, which she thought meant "mysterious," actually was more literally translated to "strange."

makes spending money on getting inked so popular among rock and roll greats looking to stain their skin with a symbol of a rockin' memory or subculture. Some of the most outrageous rocker tattoos include:

Billie Jo Armstrong (Green Day)—Circled number 27, two angels, a rose, a small cross, a vine, a baby smoking a cigar, and a tiny black heart on his right arm, as well as a baby, a clown bracelet, Jacob, a flower, and the acronym P.U.N.X. on his left arm.

Travis Barker (Blink 182)—Checkered design on both sides of his neck, "Can I Say" across his collarbone, nude women outlines on his upper chest, a radio on his stomach, and both arms sleeved with designs.

David Bowie—Lizard on his ankle.

Fatboy Slim—Smiley face with crossbones on his arm.

Kid Rock—Detroit Tigers' "D" on right arm, the name "Paul" on left bicep, a bald eagle, and the phrase "Amerian Bad Ass."

Kurt Cobain (Nirvana)—K Records logo on his arm.

Jonathan Davis (Korn)—Korn logo on his back and a bishop ripping his skin off to reveal Jesus on his right bicep.

> ### CELEBRITY ALIAS
>
> Alias: Fatboy Slim
> Actual Name: Quentin Cook, later Norman Cook

★ ★ ★ ★ ★

Wake Me Up Before You Bid

At a transatlantic auction held at the New York and London Hard Rock Cafés, **George Michael wrote a check for a staggering $2.1 million** to take home the Steinway piano John Lennon played while writing the hit single "Imagine" in the early 1970s. British tabloids reported that brothers Liam and Noel Gallagher of Oasis made bids on the historical instrument as well but quit before the bids hit a million pounds.

CELEBRITY ALIAS

Alias: George Michael
Actual Name: Georgios Panayioutou

★ ★ ★ ★ ★

If I Was A Rich Girl—Hollywood Getaways

When it's time for big stars to take a break from the Hollywood buzz, it's not a question of whether they have a vacation home to run off to— it's a question of how many and

In 2005, Lennon's handwritten sheet music and lyrics for "All You Need is Love" were bought for a whopping 600,000 pounds at a London auction.

how lavish. With nine different sandy white beaches to choose from, some stars sunbathe at the exclusive Mustique Caribbean Island—by invitation only. Who has to review and approve their application for a little R&R? Rolling Stones legend Mick Jagger. Flash a few platinum records, and he *might* let you rent the place for a cool $15 million per week. Jagger may be known for his skinny figure, but there's nothing small about his private piece of land. Tip him enough and get an over-the-top getaway getting sporty on his tennis courts and, yes, sleeping in his bed.

OTHER STARS WITH BIG BUNGALOWS

- Sting—A cozy cottage in Malibu just thirty minutes from his Hollywood mansion.
- Jennifer Lopez—A five-bedroom $5 million mansion complete with tennis courts and an infinity pool in Los Angeles.
- Shania Twain—A twenty-six-room chateau in Switzerland.

★ ★ ★ ★ ★

Psycho Cartoon Circus

It's career day at a local elementary school, and while most kids are caught up bragging about how their parents work at hospitals and beauty salons, Nick Simmons (son of KISS star Gene Simmons) is holding up a poster of his dad breathing fire and drooling blood on stage. The humor in the situation gave rocker Gene a fabulous new idea for how to spend his loads of cash—why not make a cartoon exploring the wild life of a kid whose dad is a superstar? In 2003, Simmons made the vision a reality when he created and produced *My Dad the Rock Star* for Nickelodeon. The show follows the life of twelve-year-old Willy Zilla, who has just settled down in a new hometown after touring with his dad's wild band. Complete with life lessons learned through guitar solos and a wacky New Age mother figure, the show aired alongside the likes of *Rugrats*, *Sponge Bog Square Pants*, and *Jimmy Neutron*. Simmons says the main character may look strikingly similar to his made-up psycho stage self, but insists that *most* of the show's storylines are strictly fiction.

MOMENT OF STUPIDITY

When KISS had its first big performance alongside Iggy Pop in 1974, Gene Simmons thought it would be cool to impress the audience by breathing fire. Instead, he set his hair on fire.

★ ★ ★ ★ ★

DON'T PASS ON GRASS

Just what does the multi-platinum selling Dave Matthews Band buy after hosting a rockin' concert in their hometown of Charlottesville, Virginia? A whole lot of grass. Held at the University of Virginia's stadium, the concert was packed and the damage done to the turf was so irreversible that the band had to pitch in and pay up for some new green. Before the show, the band had allegedly offered to install a special tile over the grass for protection. However, the athletic department requested the band save their dollars and just replace what they ruined after the fact.

> ### LITTLE RED CORVETTE: WHAT THE STARS ARE DRIVING
>
> Roland Gift—Saab
>
> Mick Fleetwood—Jeep
>
> Paula Abdul—Jaguar
>
> Madonna—Mercedes, Thunderbird
>
> Elvis Presley—Cadillac, Mercedes
>
> Bono—Mercedes
>
> Mike Mills—Thunderbird

★ ★ ★ ★ ★

WON'T GET CAUGHT AGAIN

British rocker Pete Townshend of The Who turned a little red when he admitted to the media that he used his credit card to enter a Web site advertising child pornography to simply "see what was there." Luckily for his reputation, the confession was in the middle of a statement he was making against the horrendous crime of exploiting children. Townshend, who was writing his autobiography about how he was sexually abused as a child, said that explicit Web sites were abhorrent and any of his further "compulsions in this area" would be to fight for child rights and ban all similar sites from the Web.

★ ★ ★ ★ ★

GUITARIST WHO ROCKS

Pete Townshend
Band: The Who
Guitar of Choice: Gibson SG Special with Hiwatt 100-watt heads
Best Known For: "Won't Get Fooled Again" on the album *Who's Next*

AND AFTER ALL, YOU'RE MY WONDER MALL

Oasis front man Noel Gallagher was all about girls, drugs, and fancy digs when his band first went mainstream with the single "Supersonic" in 1994. He even bought a whole convoy of cars, despite the fact that he has *never* had a driver's license. There is one thing, however, that Gallagher is proud to say he was never tempted to purchase—leather pants.

Oasis drummer Zak Starkey is Ringo Starr's son.

★ ★ ★ ★ ★

STINGY STAR

Frank Zappa never bought a wedding ring for his wife, Adelaide Gail. The couple got married just a few days before Zappa left for his first European tour, and his nine-month pregnant fiancée was in a bit of a hurry to shotgun the ceremony and move on with her life. Possibly the least lavish wedding of any rock star, Zappa bought a pen out of a New York City Hall vending machine (which read, "Congratulations from Mayor Lindsay"), filled out the marriage license, and headed off to Europe. In his autobiography, *The Real Frank Zappa Book*, he admits that to this day, Gail has no bling on her finger.

MOMENT OF STUPIDITY

When Frank Zappa was in the hospital for the birth of his son, the nurse hated his first choice for his new baby's name so much (Dweezil) that Zappa rattled off a long list of common male names to make her happy. The birth certificate reads "Ian Donald Calvin Euclid Zappa."

★ ★ ★ ★ ★

CAN'T SLEEP, SNAKE WILL EAT ME

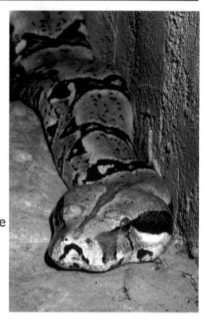

When Alice Cooper went on tour, his right-hand gal was none other than a pet boa constrictor named Veronica, who measured at about fifteen feet long. He had originally purchased the snake to take onstage as a prop, but eventually decided to let the animal accompany him in his hotel room after concerts. One day, he left Veronica lounging in his Knoxville, Tennessee, Marriott suite when she decided to take a gander down the toilet. Cooper notified management, but the snake didn't reappear for two weeks—when it crawled out and terrified singer Charlie Pride during his stay at the same hotel.

CELEBRITY ALIAS

Alias: Alice Cooper
Actual Name: Vincent Furnier

MOMENT OF STUPIDITY

Once when rehearsing for an upcoming performance with his pet boa constrictor, Evan Marie Snake, Alice Cooper was choked by it. It would not stop, and Cooper's bodyguard had to cut off its head with his pocketknife.

★ ★ ★ ★ ★

REAL ESTATE REALITY CHECK

Rap icon Nelly was test-driving a truck in Missouri in 2002 when he saw a for-sale sign and actually considered adding to his long list of riches by purchasing his own town. With hopes for his very own place to hunt and fish, he almost made the buy—but after considering it more realistically for a few minutes, he declined. For the next several weeks, however, Nelly couldn't help but daydream of how he would have called his little town Nellyville. With that fantasy in mind, Nelly made it the name of his next album.

★ ★ ★ ★ ★

ROCKERS WHO GOT RIPPED OFF

It is difficult for musicians to break into the rock and roll A-list and finally make some cash. But once they sashay down the red carpet a few times, the pressures of dropping dollars on flashy toys are tough to resist. Besides trying to keep the cash from burning a hole in their pockets, however, if stars aren't careful they can get scammed by nasty thieves looking to con a celebrity unaware. These rockers were shocked when they found out they had been duped by the best.

- Nine Inch Nails front man Trent Reznor sued ex-manager John Malm for allegedly taking millions of dollars from him after he had him sign a five-year management contract in the late 1980s. What Reznor failed to notice was that the paperwork guaranteed the managing company 20 percent of all his earnings for the rest of his career—regardless of whether they were still working together. This star should have read his contract more closely.

- When Lil' Kim lugged her luggage into New York's JFK Airport in 2003, she just couldn't keep track of the one bag full of bling. Although she intended to take her sack full of $250,000 worth of jewels on the plane with her for safekeeping, the Louis Vuitton carry-on accidentally got checked with the rest. Panicked that her diamonds had just gotten lifted, Kim had the airline hold the plane. By the time the bag was recovered, however, the jewels were long gone. One airline worker who had heard about the stolen jewels tried to cash in when he phoned and offered to give the jewelry back (which he didn't even have) for a whopping $25,000. Lucky for Kim, the idiot left her a message with his name and phone number, so that when she gave in she could give him a ring. The cops took the message instead, and he was arrested. The real jewels were later found wrapped in some rags in an airport locker.

- When a Pittsburgh identity thief charged credit cards in Will Smith's name to the tune of nearly $33,000, the star got jiggy with his lawyers and hunted down forty-two-year-old Carlos Lomax. The tip-off—Lomax had gone on a shopping spree at Sears. Assuming that Smith (or Willard C. Smith, as the credit cards read) wouldn't be caught dead at a department store, his business manager called the cops. How did the police track down the imposter? They simply looked up where he was having the goods shipped to his home.

- Young pop artist Aaron Carter fired his manager of ten years, his mother, Jane, when he was led to believe that she had taken

GUITARISTS WHO ROCK

Scotty Moore
Band: Elvis Presley's band
Guitar of Choice: Gibson ES-295 and Gibson Super 400
Best Known For: "Mystery Train" from Elvis's *The Complete Sun Sessions* (1976)

Johnny Ramone
Band: The Ramones
Guitar of Choice: Mosrite Ventures II
Best Known For: "Blitzkrieg Bop" from album *The Ramones*

David Gilmore
Band: Pink Floyd
Guitar of Choice: Fender Stratocaster
Best Known For: "Comfortably Numb" from the album *The Wall*

Steve Howe
Band: Yes
Guitar of Choice: Gibson ES-175 and a Fender Telecaster
Best Known For: "Roundabout" from the album *Fragile (1972)*

BB King
Guitar of Choice: Gibson ES-355 with a Fender Twin Reverb
Best Known For: "The Thrill is Gone" from the album *Anthology*

Albert King
Guitar of Choice: Gibson Flying V
Best Known For: "Born Under a Bad Sign" from the album of the same name

$100,000 out of his bank account without his knowing about it. Feeling a little guilty, he rehired her just one month later.

DID YOU KNOW

Guitarist Bernie Leadon of The Eagles, most famous for "Take it Easy" (1972) and "Hotel California" (1976), once dated Patti Davis, the daughter of former President Ronald Reagan. He even convinced his band mates to sing one of the songs she had written ("I Wish You Peace").

Chapter 6

Four Faces That
Shaped Rock

BO DIDDLEY

Four Faces That Shaped Rock

★ ★ ★ ★ ★ ★ ★ ★ ★ ★ ★ ★ ★ ★ ★ ★

Some early rock personalities made such an impact on the music business that it would never be the same again. They weren't all musicians, but they all had a vision for a hipper, more united rock subculture. One may not have guessed they would become such significant role models early in their lives—none came from wealthy families, and some had very little ambition. But when these early geniuses got their big break, they influenced the music industry like no one had ever done before. These are their legacies.

The American Music Awards, one of four major music award shows in the U.S., were created by Dick Clark in 1973 to compete with the Grammys.

★ ★ ★ ★ ★

THE SELF-MADE COWBOY: BILL HALEY

Getting Started—The son of a hard-working high school dropout who had taught himself to master the banjo and the mandolin, Bill Haley was kin to a small-town country music legacy. At thirteen years old, he followed in his father's self-made footsteps and learned basic chords on the guitar. The very moment he mastered it, he developed a lifelong dream to become a singing cowboy—just like in the movies. Despite his family's bleak financial situation, Haley practiced diligently and

fabulous firsts
Bill Haley and his Comets were the first American rock and roll stars to visit Great Britain.

joined a handful of local country and western bands, releasing his first record, "Candy Kisses," at just eighteen years old. He went on tour with a band of high school buddies called the Down Homers Haley, but after releasing a few unsuccessful singles in the 1940s, they went broke so quickly that Haley came crawling home, begging his mother to keep his failure a secret. Not even his fiancée, Dorothy, knew that her love had given up on fame and was sleeping off the disappointment at his parents' house.

The Turning Point—Leaving behind the dream of becoming a "singing cowboy" like Gene Autry, Haley married Dorothy, his childhood sweetheart, and became a radio show host in Chester, Pennsylvania. Bored by his twelve to sixteen-hour shifts nearly seven days a week, he decided to spice up the programming by putting together his own band to perform on the show. They were a hit, and

BILL HALEY

Date of Birth: July 6, 1925

Hometown: Highland Park, Michigan

Little Known Fact: Haley's father worked as a mechanic while his mother made 25 cents an hour giving piano lessons from home. The family was so poor that Haley's dream of becoming a singer nearly fizzled when at fifteen years old, he left school to work at a local plant bottling spring water for 35 cents an hour.

Greatest Accomplishment: In 1954, Haley's cover of Joe Turner's "Shake, Rattle, and Roll" became the first rock and roll record to sell one million copies. His next hit, "See You Later Alligator," repeated the feat—in only four weeks.

in 1950, Bill Haley and His Saddlemen cut a record of old cowboy tunes. For their next album, the band decided to change their image and put a new twist on western swing music. Their ingenuity changed the music industry forever, but the name "Saddlemen" didn't quite capture their newfound energy

and popularity. Haley remembered a cheesy nickname from a friend and applied it to the group—Bill Haley and His Comets were ready for the world.

DID YOU KNOW?

The 1956 movie *Rock Around the Clock* featured nine onscreen lip-synched performances by new artist Bill Haley, making him famous around the world.

Leaving a Legacy—Combining key elements of classic country, swing, and rhythm and blues, Bill Haley and His Comets fabricated some of the earliest rock and roll hits, including "Rock the Joint," which sold an impressive seventy-five thousand copies. Haley's next hit single, "Crazy, Man Crazy," became the first rock and roll record to make the *Billboard* pop charts, shooting to the Top 20 within weeks. It would be "Rock Around the Clock," however, that would make history and set their fame in stone. Only a partial hit at first, the song's popularity went through the roof when it was used as the title track in the cult-classic film *The Blackboard Jungle*, becoming an anthem for the nation's rebel youth. The song held *Billboard*'s No. 1 spot for eight weeks and sold 22 million copies worldwide. Haley continued to score hit singles throughout the 1950s and later starred in early rock and roll musical movies. Although his fame and fortune in the United States was eventually surpassed by a controversial young Elvis, Haley continued to be a major star in Latin America and in Europe. He died on February 9, 1981.

STUDIOS THAT SHAPED ROCK

Abbey Road

Made famous by the unforgettable Beatles album cover snapshot of Paul, Ringo, George, and John strutting their stuff down the crosswalk in 1969, Abbey Road is one of the world's most legendary streets. One of its most famed buildings of musical history is, of course, Abbey Road Studios. Originally designed for recording classical music, Abbey Road was opened in 1931 by The Gramophone Company, or EMI Records. In the beginning, though, it wasn't the swanky hangout that it is today. The first person to ever record there was the English composer Sir

Edward Elgar, who sang "The Land of Hope And Glory" with the British National Symphony Orchestra. (Snore.) Regardless of the sleepy start, however, the studio slowly acquired a host of famous connections with rock artists. When The Glen Miller Orchestra recorded its final album at Abbey Road, the studio's reputation for coolness reached the ears of Cliff Richards and the Drifters, who dropped in to cut the track for "Move It," followed by the likes of Gene Pitney, Gerry and The Pacemakers, and others. The Beatles got their start at Abbey Road Studio in 1963 with "Love Me Do" and spent the next seven years recording there. Since then, the studio has served as a recording hotspot for popular rock artists like Eric Clapton, Pink Floyd, Sting, and Oasis. It has also hosted famed composers and their orchestras recording scores for box office films including *Raiders of the Lost Ark*, *Braveheart*, and the *Lord of the Rings* trilogy.

★ ★ ★ ★ ★

THE SUBSTITUTE-TURNED-TV TALENT: DICK CLARK

Getting Started—Born Richard Wagstaff Clark in 1929, Dick Clark was infamous for his poor grades in high school—that is, until he discovered radio. A tenth grader with big dreams, Clark set his sights on broadcasting and got a job at WRUN-AM in Rome, New York, just after graduation. He was a lowly office boy without much responsibility until his boss asked him to fill in for a vacationing weatherman. Shocked to take on such an important role, he jumped at the chance for practice behind the microphone. He graduated from Syracuse University with a major in advertising and a minor in radio, then worked an array of jobs in broadcasting. In 1952, he joined WFIL radio in Philadelphia, Pennsylvania, to try his hand at an interesting new trend—deejays playing records for their listening audiences.

The Turning Point—As Clark learned how to spin records at the station, fellow deejay Bob Horn experimented with a hot new television music show called *Bandstand*. After a few episodes, Horn invited local high school students to

---

DICK CLARK
Date of Birth:
November 30, 1929

Hometown: Mount Vernon, New York

---

dance while he played music. The show was a huge success, but Horn blew it when he took a vacation and left Clark at the wheel as substitute. At just twenty-six years old, Clark was so in tune with teenagers that he quickly developed a repertoire among them, discussing the latest dance fads and clothing trends. It wasn't long before he took Horn's spot permanently. After returning from his time off, Horn was arrested for driving under the influence of alcohol and *Bandstand* producers had the confirmation they needed to pass the torch.

Leaving a Legacy—On August 5, 1957, *Bandstand* changed its name to *American Bandstand* for its first-ever national airing from 3:00 to 4:30 p.m. each day on ABC. (It later moved to Saturday.) A good balance of partying with limitations, the show had after-school entertainment value for teens and class for parents. Its famous dress code denied girls the right to wear tight clothes or slacks, and boys were asked to don a coat and tie. Calming parents' fears that rock and roll would corrupt their children, *American Bandstand* made Dick Clark and new artists like Chuck Berry, Buddy Holly, and Jerry Lee Lewis stars among the whole family. Clark stuck with the show for several decades, and when he said goodbye in 1989, it had become the longest-running program of its kind.

★ ★ ★ ★ ★

THE PIONEER MUSIC JOURNALIST: PAUL WILLIAMS

Getting Started—In the mid-1960s, those who weren't actually making music stepped up as critics to separate the good from the bad, speaking out about which stars were hot and which stars were not. The best way to share their opinions was to write about them, but where

127

could the praises and rantings be publicly read? Trade magazines like *Billboard* and *Cashbox* had long been popular, predicting which bands would flop and which would sell, but they were more known for their charts than for solid critiques. There was a hole in journalism just waiting for music critic and college student Paul Williams to step in. A freshman at Swarthmore College, just outside of Philadelphia, Williams was a science-fiction junkie familiar with the sci-fi fanzine following. He wrote a column for a local folk magazine and hosted blues programs for his college radio station.

The Turning Point—On a whim, Williams decided to start his own magazine and name it after a British club where the Rolling Stones made it big—the *Crawdaddy!* He hoped the weekly publication would provide readers with substantial musical reviews—not fluff. It was not much to look at in the beginning, though. The magazine was held together with staples, and he sold it for a quarter at record shops and bookstores from Philadelphia to New York City to Boston. *Crawdaddy!* became so popular in the northeast that he hired a handful of writers and moved the operation to an office in New York.

> **PAUL WILLIAMS**
> Birthday: May 19, 1948
>
> Hometown: Boston, Massachusetts
>
> Little Known Fact: Although *Crawdaddy!* stopped printing in 1979, Williams revived it once again for a brief twenty-eight issues in 1993. Unfortunately, financial problems forced him to put it to rest for good in 2003.

Leaving a Legacy—*Crawdaddy!* gained steam as an influence in the music industry when critical New York newspaper *The Village Voice* called it the most fascinating magazine covering the rock scene for people who "dig rock 'n' roll as an art form." It went on to influence the early years of *Rolling Stone*, a similar publication out of San Francisco. Williams quit and the magazine stopped printing for a few years, but in 1970, it returned—without its signature exclamation point and with a broader, more pop-culture approach to its articles. Sadly, the new *Crawdaddy* didn't sell as well as its former self, and shut down by 1979.

★ ★ ★ ★ ★

THE MUSICAL GENIUS: BO DIDDLEY

Getting Started—
Often described as one of the most original musical geniuses of the 1950s, Bo Diddley was born in McComb, Mississippi, in 1928. Originally named Ellas Bates, Diddley was raised by distant relatives who took him to Chicago when he was just nine years old. He took violin lessons from Ebenezer Missionary Baptist Church for twelve years, even composing two of his own concertos. The following year, his sister gave him a guitar for Christmas, and he hasn't stopped playing since. Diddley formed his own band in high school called The Hipsters

Some people believe Ellas Bates changed his name to Bo Diddley as a tribute to a slang phrase that meant "nothing," while others believe it was his nickname in the boxing ring.

(later known as The Langley Avenue Jive Cats) and began making cash landing regular gigs at the 708 Club in downtown Chicago. After graduation, he continued to play music but had to pay the bills, so he took odd jobs including truck driving and boxing.

The Turning Point—At twenty-seven years old in 1955, Diddley signed a record deal and put out his first singles, "Uncle John" and "I'm A Man." As he grew in fame with fellow artists like Chuck Berry, he became famous for influencing a rhythmic style called hambone, slapping your hands on your legs and chest while singing simple songs. Diddley became a regular at Harlem's Apollo Theatre. He was larger than life.

Leaving a Legacy—As he rose in fame, Diddley invented rock's most foundational rhythm, the "Bo Diddley beat." The popular bass line has

BO DIDDLEY

Birthday: December 30, 1928

Hometown: McComb, Mississippi

Little Known Fact: Bo Diddley was the first African American to be a guest on *The Ed Sullivan Show* on November 20, 1955. However, he and Sullivan didn't get along when he decided to sing his No. 1 hit "Bo Diddley" instead of "Sixteen Tons," as requested. He was banned from ever performing on the show again.

been picked up by decades of artists since then, including The Who, U2, and Bruce Springsteen. Diddley also gained steam as a respected artist when he designed the square-bodied cigar box guitar, one he designed for himself while at school in 1945. To this day, it is his trademark instrument. In 2005, he celebrated his fiftieth anniversary of playing music with a worldwide tour.

BO DIDDLEY SONGS COVERED BY OTHER ARTISTS:

"Who Do You Love"
—The Doors and George Thorogood

"Hey Hey" —Eric Clapton

"The Story of Bo Diddley" —The Animals

"I'm a Man"—The Yardbirds

THREE THINGS YOU NEVER KNEW ABOUT … "HAPPY BIRTHDAY"

- It was written in 1893 by two teachers in Louisville, Kentucky, originally intended as a song to greet students titled "Good Morning to All."

- The copyright is owned by Warner Communications, who purchased it for $28 million in 1985. The copyright will expire at the earliest in 2030.

- Astronauts on the Apollo IX sang "Happy Birthday" on March 8, 1969, making it the first song sung in outer space.

STUDIOS THAT SHAPED ROCK:
The Brill Building

Named after the Brill brothers, who originally built the space for their clothing store in 1931, The Brill Building is located at 1619 Broadway in the heart of New York's unique music district. When the Great Depression hit their business hard, the Brills were forced to rent out space to some of the only people still working—music publishers. Thirty years later, the department store was long gone and 165 music businesses bustled through the halls. Shoppers passing by outside could hear the smooth sounds flowing from the building onto the streets below.

In the early 1960s, The Brill Building became a one-stop-shop for anyone in the music business. There, you could write a song, then knock on a handful of doors until a publisher decided to buy it. Once you signed a contract, you could step upstairs to get your song arranged, hire a singer to record a demo, and have copies made to distribute to artists and their managers. Convince someone to make it a hit, and marketing agents were hanging around to put the record on the radio and push it to young audiences across the nation.

Chapter 7

I Heard It Through the Grapevine: Classic Rock Rumors

I Heard It Through the Grapevine: Classic Rock Rumors

★ ★ ★ ★ ★ ★ ★ ★ ★ ★ ★ ★ ★ ★ ★

Mama Cass never died choking on a ham sandwich (blame it on heart failure), and Robert Johnson never made a pact with the devil. (He was actually tutored by a blues guitarist named Ike Zimmerman.) It's tough to admit, but you have been duped. For much of your life, you have been taken for a ride by your friends, the media, and the many mistakes of oral tradition. These are just a few countless myths that have haunted the reputation of big-name celebrities for years—and it's time to face the facts. It may be tough to admit you've been wrong all this time, and let's face it, some rumors are fun to spread around. But the following tabloid treasures are just plain false.

Roy Orbison was not albino, nor was he nearly blind. His trademark glasses were simply to correct a regular vision impairment.

★ ★ ★ ★ ★

Myth #1–Paul McCartney is Dead.

On October 12, 1969, a disc jockey at WKNR-FM in Detroit broke "the news." The evidence of **the secret death of legendary Beatle Paul McCartney** was, he said, in the many clues sprinkled throughout the band's songs, artwork, and films. While dedicated fans sobbed their eyes out and lit memorial candles across the globe, the announcement was proven a hoax. However, to this day many Beatles junkies believe that the real McCartney died in a 1966 car accident while driving home from Abbey Road Studios—and that the man who claims to be him today is just a look-alike. Here's a list of why fanatics think the remaining of the Fab Four have left behind clues in their music about the fate of their beloved band mate:

- In the single "Yesterday," McCartney sings that there is a shadow hanging over him.

- In "And Your Bird Can Sing," McCartney sings, "You can't see me... You can't hear me."

- On the cover of the album *Yesterday and Today*, McCartney is sitting inside a trunk that resembles a coffin.

- On the cover for *The Yellow Submarine*, McCartney is sitting in a "sea of green," signifying being underneath the grass.

- On the cover of *Sergeant Pepper's Lonely Hearts Club Band,* a figurine of the Hindu god Shiva, also known as The Destroyer, seems to be pointing at Paul (who himself is holding a black instrument).

- On the *Abbey Road* cover, a barefoot Paul represents a dead man, John represents an angel (he is wearing white), Ringo represents the leader of a memorial service (he is wearing black), and George represents a gravedigger (he is wearing denim).

- In the song "A Day In The Life," John sings, "He blew his mind out in a car. He didn't notice that the lights had changed." Could the lyrics be a description of his friend and former band mate's death?

Regardless of how passionate believers of this popular myth may be, the band continues to stress that they are, in fact, false. Props for the creativity, though.

DID YOU KNOW

Phil Collins was an extra in The Beatles' film *A Hard Day's Night*.

★ ★ ★ ★ ★

MYTH #2 – JOAN JETT WROTE "I LOVE ROCK N' ROLL."

A rebel anthem of everything hip about rock, the song "I Love Rock N' Roll" has been recorded by a long list of musical wannabes and greats including Dragon Ash, Five, The Sex Pistols, Weird Al Yankovic, Hit Crew, and Britney Spears. The greatest myth surrounding this ever-re-recorded hit, however, is that it was originally recorded by punk guitarist Joan Jett. The song's true authors: Alan Merrill and Jake Hooker of The Arrows. After releasing two singles that raced to the top of the charts in Great Britain ("Touch Too Much" and "My Last Night With You"), The Arrows were looking to follow up their newfound fame with another big hit. Although producer Mickie Most wasn't a huge fan of the original recording and initially pushed the band to release ballad "Broken Down Heart" instead, "I

Music enthusiasts are often confused by the songwriting credits listed on the many cover versions of "I Love Rock N' Roll"— some list Alan Merrill and Jake Hooker of The Arrows as the original songwriters, while others list Allan Sachs and Jerry Mamberg. Why? Because Allan Sachs is Alan Merrill's legal name, and Jerry Mamberg is Jake Hooker's legal name.

Love Rock N' Roll" was an instant favorite after the band was invited to play it on Muriel Young's show *45* in 1975. On tour in England with her band The Runaways at the time, Joan Jett saw The Arrows' television performance and fell in love with the raw sound.

CELEBRITY ALIAS
Alias: Joan Jett Actual Name: Joan Larkin

Jett released the first cover version of "I Love Rock N' Roll" in 1979, but her adaptation wouldn't go multi-platinum until 1982—after guitarist Steve Jones and drummer Paul Cook of The Sex Pistols released *their* version of the single. In fact, despite the fact that pop-diva Britney Spears's cover has an uncanny resemblance to Jett's, representatives at Jive Records claim that while gearing up for her 2002 release, she listened to the The Arrows' original cut—not Jett's rewrite. In Great Britain, Britney's version ended up a bigger hit than Jett's—she made it to the No. 2 spot, while back in 1982, Jett just couldn't budge past No. 3.

★ ★ ★ ★ ★

MYTH #3—DIANA ROSS WAS IN THE ORIGINAL SUPREMES.

Diana Ross and soulful sidekicks Florence Ballard and Mary Wilson were not the first group to call themselves The Supremes during the early rock and roll

In 1993, Diana Ross was listed in *The Guinness Book of World Records* as the most successful female artist ever.

era of the 1950s and 1960s. In 1957, a group from Columbus, Ohio, released a single called "Just You and I" under the band name The Supremes. The 1963 hit "Our Day Will Come" was sung by a second group of the same name that was originally Ruby and the Romantics.

★ ★ ★ ★ ★

MYTH #4–MARILYN MANSON ACTED ON THE WONDER YEARS.

From 1988-1993, every little girl with a crush on Kevin Arnold would have given anything to be his beautiful sidekick (and first kiss) Winnie Cooper on sitcom *The Wonder Years*. The same girls got nauseous, however, when they heard the unthinkable rumor that Marilyn Manson (or Brian Warner, as his parents called him) starred as the geeky, allergy-ridden Paul Pfeiffer on the same show. How could such a loyal friend and nerd turn out to be someone as rebellious and sickly satanic as Manson? When confronted with the nasty myth his cult-fans were spreading across the nation, the mysterious rocker left them without much of an answer, saying it was "irrelevant" as to whether or not the rumor was true.

However, fans can breathe a sigh of relief because Paul Pfeiffer was not played by Marilyn Manson but instead by Josh Saviano, a young actor who also made frequent appearances on children's shows like *Reading Rainbow* and *Fun House*. A graduate of Yale University, today Saviano is a lawyer. Manson has also dodged rumors that he played the innocent, good-hearted Charlie Bucket in the quirky film *Willy Wonka and the Chocolate Factory* with Gene Wilder—that, too, is not true.

★ ★ ★ ★ ★

Myth #5—Creed Is a Christian Band.

As a teenager, Scott Stapp wanted to prove to his parents so badly that rock music wasn't the antithesis of religion that he eventually ran away from home. Years later as a student at Lee University, a Christian liberal-arts college, he was kicked out for smoking marijuana. A rocker raised on faith and his own love for rock and roll, Stapp was so inspired by the tunes of Led Zeppelin that he got together with some high school buddies from Tallahassee, Florida, and put together the band Creed and its premier album *My Own Prison*. At first they were criticized for their predictably Christian lyrics in singles like "My Sacrifice" and "With Arms Wide Open," but none of the band members ever openly admitted any kind of personal religious commitment. Similar to U2, the guys denied being a "Christian band" but still wanted to sing about their religious thoughts and questions in their music.

What many of the band's anti-religion enemies do not know, however, is that Stapp wrote those seemingly Christian lyrics while questioning the very faith he was raised on—in fact, in more than one interview, he admitted that *My Own Prison* wasn't referencing a specific God at all. He didn't want to directly support a Christian God or a Muslim God or a Buddhist God. His God was just the God he "saw in nature," he said. At the height of making music in the 1990s, Stapp refused to even call himself a Christian because of all the theological problems he had with the faith. USA Today may have called Creed "Bible thumping rockers," but they would claim otherwise. Whether Stapp denies or openly admits any form of faith today, his music has had a positive effect on fans, driving them toward the possibility of hope and heaven.

★ ★ ★ ★ ★

MYTH #6-"AMERICAN PIE" IS NAMED AFTER BUDDY HOLLY'S FALLEN PLANE.

On February 3, 1959, Buddy Holly, Ritchie Valens, and J.P. Richardson drew straws with their road crew to see who had to ride in the steamy, un-air-conditioned tour bus and who got to hitch a ride on the airplane. The three young stars won, but their fate would change when their four-passenger Beechcraft Bonanza crashed into a snowy Iowa cornfield at 1:05 a.m.

CELEBRITY ALIAS

Alias: Buddy Holly
Actual Name: Charles
Hardin Holley

Twelve years later, Don McLean wrote the ballad "American Pie" as a tribute to the ill-fated rock heroes, making February 3rd the unofficial "day the music died." However, some music lovers took the tribute too far when they spread the rumor that "American Pie" was actually the name of the fallen airplane. The claim is simply not true.

★ ★ ★ ★ ★

MYTH #7–JACK AND MEG WHITE ARE SIBLINGS.

Although they had been playing together since 1999, when punk garage band White Stripes first became widely noticed with the single "Fell in Love With a Girl" in 2001, they had fooled music lovers with the legend that they were brother and sister. Claiming to be the youngest of a family of ten, the duo did share pasty white skin and jet-black hair. However, they were not blood relatives—they were married. In 2001, a reporter revealed the fact that Megan White and John (Jack) Gillis had actually been wed from 1996-2001. Today copies of their divorce papers circle the Web, telling the true tale of their relationship.

★ ★ ★ ★ ★

MYTH #8–BLACK SABBATH IS NAMED AFTER A WITCHES' GATHERING.

Rumors of gothic references to the occult in band names and lyrics are nothing new to the rock scene. In fact, some bands like the mystery and controversy that comes with such confusion. With dark onstage performances by the wild and questionable Ozzy Osbourne, it was easy for Black Sabbath fans to believe the myth that their favorite rockers were a tribute to witchcraft. However, the band's name actually comes from their love of horror flicks—one in particular, the 1963 *Black Sabbath* starring Boris Karloff. Since retiring, Ozzy has appeared on a number of talk shows explaining that the band's act was not satanic but mere theater.

★ ★ ★ ★ ★

Myth #9—Michael Jackson Does ... Just About Everything.

The King of Pop has pulled off quite a few cheesy stunts in his day. He performed at the 1996 BRIT Awards dressed as the Messiah, surrounded by kids and a mock rabbi. He outbid a good friend (Paul McCartney) for ownership of The Beatles' catalog of songs. As a grown man, he purchased a California ranch, filled it with amusement park rides and zoo animals, and named it Neverland.

Despite his addiction to utterly weird ways, Jackson is a misunderstood man surrounded by countless rumors, including:

- He sleeps in a pressure chamber to prevent aging. Anyone who paid attention to his 2005 lawsuit and trial knows Jackson clearly sleeps in a bed. It should be whether he has company that is up for question.

- He purposefully lightened his skin because he hates being black. Jackson actually has a condition called vitiligo, which causes pigment to fade away, leaving behind white splotches.

fabulous firsts

"Billie Jean" by Michael Jackson was the first video by a black artist to air on MTV.

- He purchased the remains of "Elephant Man" Joseph Merrick. The actual organs were destroyed during World War II. Jackson may have visited the Royal London Hospital to view casts of Merrick's head and appendages, but he certainly never took them home.

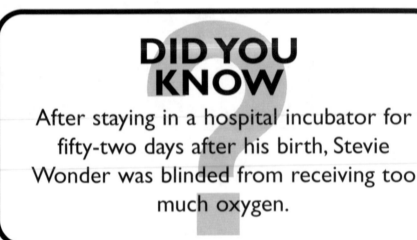

DID YOU KNOW

After staying in a hospital incubator for fifty-two days after his birth, Stevie Wonder was blinded from receiving too much oxygen.

Chapter 8

Famous Firsts
and Origins

IN THE
BEGINNING

Famous Firsts and Origins

★ ★ ★ ★ ★ ★ ★ ★ ★ ★ ★ ★ ★ ★ ★ ★

Just what inspired ingenious songwriters to pen their famous lyrics, and how did bands like The Ramones and 10,000 Maniacs come up with their stage names? Take an inside look into these origins, as well as famous firsts, such as the first music video and first model of the electric guitar. You might be surprised at the stories behind these classic rock origins.

fabulous firsts

The first *Billboard* chart, introduced in 1936 as Chart Line, listed the most-played songs on three radio networks.

★ ★ ★ ★ ★

THE ORIGIN OF ... ROCK AND ROLL'S MOST FAMOUS LYRICS

The Song: "Tutti Frutti"

The Artist: Little Richard

The Story: Richard coined the phrase "a-wop-bop-a-loo-bop-a-lop-bam-boom" while working as a dishwasher.

The Song: "My Boyfriend's Back"

The Artist: The Angels

The Story: While working as a songwriter for April-Blackwood music in 1963, Bob Feldman caught word that his favorite Brooklyn Sweet Shoppe (located across the street from his old high school) was going to be torn down. While paying it one last visit, Feldman overheard a young girl arguing with a hoodlum-looking young man outside. "My boyfriend's back in town, and you're gonna be in trouble," she screamed. Laughing at the episode with friends later that night, Feldman penned the No. 1 song "My Boyfriend's Back" for The Angels.

The Song: "You Ain't Seen Nothin' Yet"

The Artist: Bachman-Turner Overdrive

The Story: When Randy Bachman first practiced the "b-b-b-baby" in the single "You Ain't Seen Nothin' Yet," he was making fun of his brother, Gary, who had a problem with stuttering. The band laughed at the mockery at first but later realized it was a golden idea for the chorus.

The Song: "I Saw the Light"

The Artist: Todd Rundgren

The Story: The lyrics to the 1972 single "I Saw the Light" came so quickly to Todd Rundgren that he vowed to never write that rapidly again—if it only takes fifteen minutes, it will end up as nothing more than a string of stupid clichés. To this day, Rundgren thinks the song is rubbish.

The Song: "Sweet Home Alabama"

The Artist: Lynyrd Skynyrd

The Story: Guitarist Gary Rossington had a bone to pick with Neil Young in the 1970s for dissing the South in his single "Southern Man." As a joke to retaliate and fix the damage done to the South's surly reputation, Lynyrd Skynyrd wrote "Sweet Home Alabama," *never* expecting it to be a hit or even a single.

DID YOU KNOW?

Stevie Wonder, born Steveland Morris, wrote "Isn't She Lovely" in honor of his daughter Aisha Zakia, whose name means "strength" and "intelligence" in a native African language.

DID YOU KNOW

Gladys Knight's hit song "Midnight Train to Georgia" was originally written as "Midnight Plane to Houston."

The Song: "Running on Empty"
The Artist: Jackson Browne
The Story: Singer/songwriter Jackson Browne drove back and forth from his home to the recording studio so often that he really didn't feel like changing his

route to find a gas station when the tank flirted with "E." Praying that the car would get him home from work one day, Browne randomly started humming the tune that would later become the melody for the new song titled "Running on Empty."

The Song: "Proud Mary"
The Artist: Credence Clearwater Revival
The Story: John Fogerty wrote the song "Proud Mary" in the midst of a joyful celebration after he opened a letter that said he had been discharged from the army.

The Song: "That'll Be the Day"
The Artist: Buddy Holly
The Story: Sang by Buddy Holly and Jerry Allison in their hip new band The Crickets, "That'll Be The Day" was inspired by a John Wayne film called *The Searchers* in which a loner cowboy sneers the phrase, "That'll be the day."

The Song: "You're in My Heart"
The Artist: Rod Stewart
The Story: Stewart says many women may think he wrote "You're in My Heart" as a tribute to them, but in reality, it's a reflection on all the loves of his

life—soccer, football, Scotland, his parents, and maybe two or three different women he has swooned over the years.

MOMENT OF STUPIDITY

When Rod Stewart first performed at the Filmore East in New York in 1968, he was so nervous that he sang his first song from backstage.

The Song: "Aqualung"
The Artist: Jethro Tull
The Story: After mulling over some photographs his wife had taken of a homeless man, front man Ian Anderson came up with "Aqualung" as a tribute to spiritual equality. Regardless of how low the man in the photograph may be labeled, he says, there is still a piece of God inside him.

The Song: "Daniel"

The Artist: Elton John

The Story: Songwriter Bernie Taupin read a story in a national newsmagazine about a wounded soldier from Vietnam who wanted to settle back into his average life but was treated like such a hero that he had to leave the U.S. to get some peace and quiet. It was that article that inspired him to write "Daniel" for Elton John, who recorded it the very same day.

The Song: "Heartbreak Hotel"

The Artist: Elvis

The Story: When the *Miami Herald* printed a suicide note for the public to read in conjunction with one of their top news stories, Elvis took one look at it and was inspired enough to pen the lyrics to "Heartbreak Hotel."

CELEBRITY ALIAS

Alias: Elton John
Actual Name: Reginald Dwight

MOMENTS OF STUPIDITY

Elton John has appeared in concert dressed as:

Donald Duck
Prince Charming
Mozart
Ronald McDonald
Uncle Sam
Santa Claus

THREE THINGS YOU NEVER KNEW ABOUT ... ELVIS

- He had an identical twin brother named Garon who died at birth. Elvis honored him with the middle name Aron.

- He loved to visit the morgues in Memphis to "check out the corpses."

- He was not the first artist to record "Blue Suede Shoes"—Carl Perkins recorded it for Sun Records.

154

The Song: "Brand New Key"

The Artist: Melanie

The Story: Songwriter Melanie Safka was a hopeless vegetarian until she gave into temptation and downed a McDonald's hamburger one day in the early 1970s. All stomachaches aside, the meal was a good move, because just after she ate, she came up with the hit song "Brand New Key."

The Song: "Layla"

The Artist: Eric Clapton

The Story: When Clapton wrote "Layla," he was lusting after Beatle George Harrison's wife, Patti, whom he had met when she was just nineteen years old on the set of *A Hard Day's Night*. Desperately in love with a woman who refused to leave her husband, Clapton wrote the Top 10 single as a tribute to his broken heart.

DID YOU KNOW

While a young musician struggling to make it big, Billy Joel recorded a pretzel commercial with Chubby Checker.

★ ★ ★ ★ ★

THE DAY THE MUSIC DIED (AND ROSE AGAIN): THE ORIGIN OF ... THE ROCK ERA

When WWII peaked as a major conflict, the swingin' Big Band era came to a halting end. Musicians enrolled in the armed forces, the American Federation of Music went on strike, and clubs dishing out their dues to wartime taxes had to shut their doors for good. For those who did stick it out in the music business, touring was hardly an option, thanks to the rationing of tires, gas, and other materials. By the time fighting came to an end, teenagers took life pretty seriously. Straight-laced with nothing to look forward to but a forty-hour workweek, they were too busy with the daily grind to mess around with music—but not for long.

Enter the 1950s—the economy is booming and parents, who were bored to tears during their own childhoods, are suddenly eager to live vicariously through their kids by pushing them to the party scene. Spending more time out with friends than ever before, youngsters finally started making decisions for themselves. With their newfound freedom (and newfound allowances), they had the power and the cash to make an impact on the music biz. In the October 13, 1958, edition of *Billboard* magazine, singer Jo Strafford commented on the turnaround. "Today's 9- to 14-year-old group is the first generation with enough money

> In the 1950s, "cats" became a nickname for white teens who listened to traditionally black jazz tunes.

THE EARLY YEARS

- When Paul Anka was fifteen years old, he wrote the 1957 No. 1 hit "Diana" as a poetic tribute to his younger sibling's babysitter, who was older than he and had no romantic interest in him whatsoever.

- Malcolm Angus of AC/DC once worked as a maintenance man in a bra factory. A mechanic, he fixed sewing machines when they broke down.

- Before they were famous, Sonny and Cher were known as Cleo and Caesar.

- Eddie Van Halen played guitar on Michael Jackson's hit single "Beat It."

- Guns N Roses' Axl Rose (aka Billy Bailey and William Bruce Rose) was infamous with the police as a teenager in Indiana. He was put in jail more than twenty times. He must have held a grudge, because when he returned to his home state to play a concert in 1991, he compared his hometown to Auschwitz.

- When auditioning for a record deal in England in 1967, The Bee Gees sang a set of three songs that included "Puff the Magic Dragon." Executive Robert Stigwood was appalled and left the room, but later reconsidered and signed them to his label.

- At twenty-two years old, Barry Manilow, born Barry Alan Pinkus, had a letter printed in *Playboy* magazine asking editors for advice on how to start a successful music career. Their reply: "Go sow your wild musical notes." It doesn't get any wilder than "Copacabana."

given to them by their parents to buy records in sufficient quantities," he said. "In my youth, if I asked my father for 45 cents to buy a record, he'd have thought seriously about having me committed."

The freedom for teens to party hard would come at a price—they would all end up grounded. A lot. The more they dropped dollars on records and dance clubs, the more they clashed with their parents about music—which (according to the media and to most adults) was the ultimate road to eternal damnation and juvenile delinquency. In the end, teens bought their own radios, ran off to a random field (think *Footloose*), and joined the rockabilly, swivel-hip dancing of Elvis Presley and Jerry Lee Lewis.

★ ★ ★ ★ ★

THE ORIGIN OF ... THE TERM "ROCK AND ROLL"

History buffs often disagree on who first coined the term "rock and roll" (and from what song the phrase got its inspiration). While most accounts credit Cleveland disc jockey Alan Freed, who certainly gave America's population its first taste of the expression, others insist the term had been around for decades before. But what did it insinuate before it classified a type of music? Originally, the term was a bit of a blues double entendre, referencing both saints and sinners—religion and sex. Some of its earliest uses date back to nautical phrases used by sailors in

Alan Freed may have introduced the term "rock and roll" to listening audiences across America, but most rock historians dispute what song first inspired him to do so. Some say "Sixty Minute Man" by The Dominoes, while others say "My Baby Rocks Me with a Steady Roll" by Rumba Caliente.

the 1600s (referring to the sway of a ship, or possibly the sway of a woman's hips). African Americans often referred to rocking as a euphoric religious experience accompanied by powerful music, so the word "rock" made its way into spiritual music and gospel lyrics like "rock my soul in the bosom of Abraham," "rock me Jesus" and "rock me in the cradle of Thy love."

★ ★ ★ ★ ★

THE ORIGIN OF ... THE FIRST CROSSOVER ALBUM

When it comes to boosting record sales, nothing is more effective than tapping into the tastes of multiple fan bases (think Jessica Simpson goes *Dukes of Hazzard*). In the 1990s, Faith Hill and Shania Twain were transformed from down-home Country Music Television (CMT) mammas to VH1 sex symbols nearly overnight. Latin pop diva Shakira became an American icon when she dyed her brown locks blonde and released her first English album, *Laundry Service,* in 2001. The first crossover albums, however, were released in the 1950s when black vocalists suddenly became famous as doo-wop evolved into an early form of rock. Traditional jazz groups like The Dominoes and Midnighters had new audiences, and independent recording companies couldn't believe their ears when they heard that black artists were actually selling records to white teenagers. (Scandalous!)

★ ★ ★ ★ ★

ORIGIN OF ... THE PHONOGRAPH

Folklore tells the story of how Thomas Edison first had his idea for the phonograph when a train conductor yanked him onto a locomotive by his ears. As much as that might have jarred his brain to work, it was more likely Edison's disability, mastoiditis, and his astonishment with buddy Alexander Graham Bell's telephone that led him to design the first version of his "talking machine." Partnering with his associate Charles Batchelor and machinist John Kruesi, in less than a year Edison was wowing the staff of *Scientific American* with the first gadget to ever record sounds/speech. Initially more of a business tool than a form of entertainment, the Talking Machine ended up costing way too much for the average citizen to afford. Plus, the little strip of tinfoil that taped the speeches wore out after just one or two uses (and took a ridiculous amount of

fabulous firsts

The first annual Grammy Awards were awarded in 1959. The Record of the Year was *Volare* by Domenico Modugno, the Album of the Year went to Peter Gunn by Henry Mancini, and the winner of the best R&B performance was "Tequila" by Champs.

work to replace). One headache after another, the original phonograph flopped—it was one of Edison's worst-selling inventions.

★ ★ ★ ★ ★

THE ORIGIN OF ... THE JUKEBOX

Edison's original phonograph company may have been a nightmare, but at least one of his employees hit the big time after the fact. **Louis Glass, who had once worked for Edison, had a genius idea for how to jazz up his former boss's invention.** Why not record a handful of hits on the (new and improved) phonograph and stick a coin box on the side to make money every time someone wanted to play a song? Glass put the new creation in San Francisco's Palais Royal Saloon, and the jukebox was born. Two things that made it a huge success:

The jukebox got its name from two sources. The word Jook is an old African-American term meaning to dance (or to dance sexually). The word Juke, on the other hand, is a spoof on lower-class bars called juke joints that were frequented by Southern jute field workers at the end of a long, hot harvest.

- **Alcohol.** When the Automatic Music Instrument Company created the world's first "electrically amplified multi-selection phonograph," or jukebox, in 1927, it was Prohibition that caused initial sales to skyrocket. Underground speakeasy joints loved the product because they needed music to keep their guests around, but could never afford to pay a live band to play in such a dank place.

- **Racists.** The jukebox was considered "color blind in a segregated world." When black clientele at local bars heard the popular tunes of Bill Black, Carl Perkins, and Steve Cropper, they assumed they were black artists and showed them great respect. Similarly, whites more easily accepted and enjoyed black musicians' music when they could listen to it without seeing the live performance.

THREE THINGS YOU NEVER KNEW ABOUT... THE JUKEBOX

- While some people believed jukebox-manufacturing company Rock-Ola was named after the rise of rock and roll, it was actually named after the company's founder, Canadian David Rockola.

- The Wurlitzer 1946 model 1015 jukebox was the most popular of the 1940s era. It toted the slogan, "Wurlitzer Is Jukebox."

- From 1942-1946, the United States government called off jukebox production to preserve labor and materials for the war effort.

★ ★ ★ ★ ★

THE ORIGIN OF ... THE ELECTRIC GUITAR

Some say Nat King Cole was among the first to start the rock and roll phenomenon with his 1942 *Jazz at the Philharmonic* single titled "Blues Part 2." Others would say it was the later works of Chuck Berry, Carl Perkins, and Big Joe Turner. Regardless, the invention of the solid-body electric guitar changed the future of rock as we know it.

Les Paul (formerly known as Lester Polfus in his hometown of Waukesha, Wisconsin) knew the value of a guitar—he had been playing since he was a boy, starting out on a Sears and Roebuck Gene Autry model that cost him $5. Hungry for a little extra cash, Paul performed in drive-in hamburger joints but realized that his music was too muffled for everyone making out in the back row to hear. So he turned his radio into a PA system to help amplification. When that wasn't enough, he decided to simply build a louder guitar.

PACK RAT FEVER

Les Paul kept all his memorabilia from the early days of designing guitars. He still has his first amplifier and PA system (an Atwater Kent radio).

Paul's first version of the solid-body electric guitar was a needle and a cartridge attached to his original acoustic. To keep the feedback down, he stuffed it with rags and plaster of Paris. A few versions later, the final product was the renowned commercial version of the Les Paul electric guitar. Since then, Paul's work has been so respected that he has designed models for industry suppliers such as Gibson.

★ ★ ★ ★ ★

ORIGIN OF ... COOL BAND NAMES

- Wild Cherry, the band that sang the disco hit "Play that Funky Music," is named after a box of cough drops.

- Duran Duran took its band name from the 1968 film *Barbarella*.

- Rocker Adam Ant came up with his pseudonym after laughing at the British sitcom *Adam Adamant Lives!*

- Bo Diddley, born Utha Ellas Bates McDaniel, is rumored to have named himself after a unique African guitar.

- Elvis Costello, whose real name is declan Patrick Aloysius McManus, put together his stage name to honor the famed Elvis Presley and his mother (whose maiden name was Costello).

MOMENT OF STUPIDITY

The Ramones had the cops called on them by a Rhode Island club owner for walking out after only playing for twenty minutes. The band argued that they had played a full set of twenty-two songs; they just did it more quickly than usual.

- The Ramones renamed themselves in honor of Paul McCartney's former alias, Paul Ramon. Their real names are Douglas Colvin (Dee Dee), Jeffrey Hyman (Joey), John Cummings (Johnny), Richard Beau (Richie), Marc Bell (Marky), and Thomas Erdelyi (Tommy).

- Moby named himself after his relative Herman Melville's acclaimed novel *Moby Dick*.

- Conway Twitty coined his name after a couple of small towns in Arkansas.

- 10,000 Maniacs were inspired by the horror flick *2000 Maniacs*.

MOMENT OF STUPIDITY

British rockers Depeche Mode took their name from the French phrase that translates to "fast fashion." Those who didn't like the band often teased them with the nickname Depede Mode, which means "dirty pedophiles."

- The Black Crowes were originally Uncle Crowe's Garden, a tribute to a fairy tale.

- ABBA is an acronym for the band members' first names: Agnetha, Bjorn, Benny, and Anni-Frid.

- Radiohead came up with its name after listening to a Talking Heads song called "Radio Head."

- Despite rumors that Eddie Vedder's delicious jam-making grandmother was named Pearl, rockers Pearl Jam got their name from the natural process by which wastes from the ocean are made into beautiful jewels.

★ ★ ★ ★ ★

MORE CELEBRITY ALIASES FROM A TO Z

Alias: Tori Amos
Actual Name: Myra Ellen Amos

Alias: Andre 3000 of Outkast
Actual Name: Benjamin Andre

Alias: Babyface
Actual Name: Kenneth Brian Edmonds

Alias: Bobby Day
Actual Name: Robert Byrd

Alias: Mickey Dolenz
Actual Name: George Michael Braddock

Alias: Gloria Estefan
Actual Name: Gloria Fajardo

Alias: Enya
Actual Name: Eithne ni Bhraonain

Alias: Fish
Actual Name: Derek William Dick

Alias: Leif Garrett
Actual Name: Leif Per Narvik

Alias: Boy George
Actual Name: George O'Dowd

Alias: Richard Hell
Actual Name: Richard Meyers

Alias: Billy Idol
Actual Name: William Board

Alias: Iggy Pop
Actual Name: James Jewel Osterberg Jr.

Alias: Rick James
Actual Name: James Ambrose Johnson

Alias: Alicia Keys
Actual Name: Alicia Augello Cook

Alias: Chaka Khan
Actual Name: Yvette Marie Stevens

Alias: Huey Lewis
Actual Name: Hugh Cregg

Alias: Courtney Love
Actual Name: Love Michelle Harrison

Alias: Meatloaf
Actual Name: Marvin Lee Aday

Alias: Freddie Mercury
Actual Name: Farrokh Bulsara

Alias: Billy Ocean
Actual Name: Leslie Sebastian Charles

Alias: Pink
Actual Name: Alecia Moore

Alias: Queen Latifah
Actual Name: Dana Owens

Alias: Terminator X (Public Enemy)
Actual Name: Norman Lee Rogers

Alias: Tina Turner
Actual Name: Annie Mae Bullock

Alias: Vanilla Ice
Actual Name: Robert van Winkle

★ ★ ★ ★ ★

THE ORIGIN OF THE MONKEES

When record company executives were looking for a couple of wacky, longhaired musicians to play in a new television show called *The Monkees* in 1965, they put an ad in two American newspapers that read: "Madness! Folk and Roll Musicians-Singers for acting roles in new TV series. Running parts for four insane boys, age 17 to 21." The new sitcom band was considered so dreamy among young teenage girls that the boys were invited to choose a few songs to record for a real record. They may have been

---

HAIR TODAY, GONE TOMORROW

In several second-season episodes of *The Monkees* television series, Micky's hairstyle switches back and forth from straight to curly because half of the episodes were filmed in the spring of 1967 and the rest were filmed later that fall.

---

one of the most popular groups of their time, but they didn't have much savvy when it came to song selection—they turned down "Knock Three Times," which later became a huge hit for Tony Orlando and Dawn in 1970, and "Love Will Keep Us Together," which sold more than a million records for The Captain and Tennille in 1975.

DID YOU KNOW

The only mother and son to have No. 1 hits on the Billboard Hot 100 are Shirley Jones of the Partridge Family ("I Think I Love You" in 1970) and Shaun Cassidy ("Da Do Ron Ron Ron" in 1977).

★ ★ ★ ★ ★

Video Killed the Radio Star: The Origin of ... MTV...

On August 1, 1981, every ugly singer's stomach sank when the Music Television Network aired its first flick, "Video Killed the Radio Star," by the Buggles. What was once a form of audio entertainment now required a new element—hotness. MTV was the brainchild of James Lack and Bob Pittman, who had previously worked with Nickelodeon and dreamed up a number of musical children's series that never quite made the cut. How did producers switch gears to tap into teenager's rebel mindsets and reel them in to the program? They let Sting and Pat Benatar do it in bits on other youth-oriented networks featuring the rockers screaming, "I want my MTV!" With six hot young deejays standing by to take requests, the ploy did well—and the videos did

CELEBRITY ALIAS

Alias: Pat Benatar
Actual Name: Patricia Andrejewski

even better as they managed to keep the attention of impatient young teens with remote controls. After two years, MTV had increased the number of cable companies carrying its channel by 600 percent. Sixteen million homes were tuning in.

As groundbreaking as MTV was during its first few years of syndication, the early music videos weren't what they are today. They were sort of like choppy commercials for upcoming record releases. In fact, before the term "music video" came out, the three-to-four minute clips of singing and dancing were often called "promotional clips." MTV did one thing for American music lovers in the end—they proved that a good video could make a terrible song a huge hit.

fabulous firsts

MTV's five original veejays were Martha Quinn, Mark Goodman, Alan Hunter, Nina Blackwood, and J.J. Jackson.

MOMENT OF STUPIDITY

Dionne Warwick's birth name was actually Marie Dionne Warrick—but a spelling error on her first album in 1962 forced her to get used to the alternate spelling. Ever the psychic, she added an "e" to the end after being advised to do so by a numerologist, but it never stuck.

Where We Got This Stuff

Associated Press, "Rock and Roll hall sues Jewish rock hall." *MSNBC*, February 8, 2005, http://msnbc.msn.com/id/6936995/

Bathroom Readers' Hysterical Institute. *Uncle John's Bathroom Reader Plunges Into Great Lives*. San Diego: Portable Press, 2003.

Bathroom Reader's Institute. *Uncle John's 4-Ply Bathroom Reader*. New York: Barnes & Noble Books, 1991.

Beasley, Jake. *Celebrity Aliases Unmasked*. USA: Sweetwater Press, 2004.

Bordowitz, Hank. *Turning Points in Rock and Roll*. New York: Kensington Publishing Corporation, 2004.

Clarke, John. *The Greatest Rock and Pop Miscellany Ever!* Italy: Sanctuary Publishing, 2004.

Cloud, David W. "The Religious Affiliation of Rock and Roll Star Buddy Holly." *Adherents.com*, July 19, 2005, http://www.adherents.com/people/ph/Buddy_Holly.html

——. "The Religious Affiliation of Rock and Roll Star Roy Orbison." *Adherents.com*, July 19, 2005, http://www.adherents.com/people/po/Roy_Orbison.html

D'Angelo, Joe. "Dave Matthews Buys Grass for University of Virginia." *VH1.com*, www.vh1.com/artists/az/dave_ matthews_band/news.jhtml?p=76&q=25

Joseph, Mark. *The Rock and Roll Rebellion*. Nashville: Broadman & Holman Publishers, 1999.

Joseph, Mark. *Faith, God and Rock and Roll*. Grand Rapids: Baker Books, 2003.

Kitts, Jeff, and Brad Tolinski, eds. *Guitar World Presents: Greatest Guitarists of All Time!* Milwaukee: Hal Leonard Corporation, 2002.

Melloan, Maryanne. *Rock and Roll Revealed: The Outrageous Lives of Rock's Biggest Stars*. New York: Smithmark, 1993.

Morse, Tim. *Classic Rock Stories*. New York: St. Martin's Griffin, 1998.

Moser, Margaret, and Bill Crawford. *Rock Stars Do the Dumbest Things*. New York: St. Martin's Griffin, 1998.

Palmer, Robert. "Copyright Nightmare Haunts Bee Gees," *New York Times*, April 6, 1983.

Patel, Joseph. "P. Diddy Cleared In Lawsuit Brought by TV Interviewer." *MTV.com*, February 24, 2004, http://www.mtv.com/news/articles/1485297/20040224/p_diddy.jhtml?headlines=true

Patterson, R. Gary. *Take A Walk on the Dark Side: Rock and Roll Myths, Legends, and Curses.* New York: Simon & Schuster, 2004.

Petras, Kathryn and Ross. *Unusually Stupid Americans.* New York: Villard Books, 2003.

Reid, Shaheem. "Impulse Shopper Nelly Nearly Purchases a Small Town." *VH1.com,* March 19, 2002, www.vh1.com/artists/az/nelly/news.jhtml?p=126&q=25

Shea, Stuart. *Rock and Roll's Most Wanted.* Washington D.C.: Brassey's, Inc, 2002.

Sullivan, James. "Rock's 10 Wildest Myths." *Rolling Stone,* October 12, 2004, http://www.rollingstone.com/rsmyth

Thompson, Graeme. "The 10 Greatest Rock'n'Roll Myths." *The Observer,* February 20, 2005, http://observer.guardian.co.uk

Turner, Steve. *Hungry for Heaven: Rock 'n' Roll and the Search for Redemption.* Illinois: InterVarsity Press, 1995.

Zappa, Frank. *The Real Frank Zappa Book.* New York: Touchstone Books, 1989.

WE ALSO USED THESE SOURCES:

www.beliefnet.com

www.cbsnews.com

www.chartattack.com

www.classicbands.com

www.corsinet.com

www.cnn.com

www.digitaldreamdoor.com

www.eonline.com

www.fiftiesweb.com

www.foxnews.com

www.hinduismtoday.com

www.history-of-rock.com

www.jewsrock.org

www.jokesnjokes.net

www.leftlion.co.uk

www.legalzoom.com

www.memphisrocknsoul.org

www.news.com

www.rockhall.com

www.vh1.com

www.wikipedia.org

mental_floss magazine

ABOUT THE AUTHOR

Camille Smith Platt is a freelance writer and the Editor of *Chattanooga Christian Family* magazine. A graduate of the Samford University Department of Journalism and Mass Communication, she has also done research and writing for national trivia magazine *mental_floss* and Birmingham lifestyle magazine *PORTICO*. Her love-hate relationship with trivia stems from a fascination of quirky knowledge and a lifetime of always being stumped. She and her husband, Daniel, live in Chattanooga, Tennessee.

YOU MAY ALSO ENJOY THESE OTHER BOOKS IN THE REAL CHEESY SERIES.

Real Cheesy Facts About: U.S. Presidents

ISBN-13: 978-1-57587-248-3

ISBN-10: 1-57587-248-X

Real Cheesy Facts About: TV & Movies

ISBN-13: 978-1-57587-249-0

ISBN-10: 1-57587-249-8

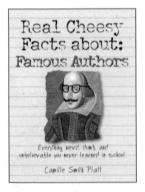

Real Cheesy Facts About: Famous Authors

ISBN-13: 978-1-57587-250-6

ISBN-10: 1-57587-250-1